AFTER GANDHI

ONE HUNDRED YEARS OF NONVIOLENT RESISTANCE

AFTER GANDHI

ONE HUNDRED YEARS OF NONVIOLENT RESISTANCE

Anne Sibley O'Brien and
Perry Edmond O'Brien

ini Charlesbridge

For the Gandhi Publishing team,
with appreciation and hope

Published by Charlesbridge
85 Main Street
Watertown, MA 02472
(617) 926-0329
www.charlesbridge.com

Library of Congress Cataloging-in-Publication Data
O'Brien, Anne Sibley.
    After Gandhi : one hundred years of nonviolent resistance / Anne Sibley
O'Brien and Perry Edmond O'Brien; illustrated by Anne Sibley O'Brien.
        p. cm.
    Includes bibliographical references.
    ISBN 978-1-58089-129-5 (reinforced for library use)
1. Passive resistance. 2. Nonviolence. I. O'Brien, Perry Edmond. II. Title.
HM1281.O33 2009
303.6'1—dc22   2008010660

Printed in the United States of America
(hc) 10 9 8 7 6 5 4 3 2 1

Illustrations done in water-soluble pastels
Display type set in Croteau; text type set in Sabon
Art preparation by Chroma Graphics, Singapore
Printed and bound by Courier
Production supervision by Brian G. Walker
Designed by Susan Mallory Sherman

CONTENTS

Delano

Birmingham
Montgomery
Houston

Belfast

Buenos Aires

Prague

Beijing

Rural Vietnam

A Village
in Burma

Nairobi

Johannesburg

Cape Town

Moree

A SMALL BODY OF DETERMINED SPIRITS FIRED BY AN UNQUENCHABLE FAITH IN THEIR MISSION CAN ALTER THE COURSE OF HISTORY. MOHANDAS GANDHI

INTRODUCTION

ON AUGUST 16, 1908, in Johannesburg, South Africa, a lawyer from India named Mohandas Gandhi spoke to a crowd of more than three thousand. These Indian men he had helped organize were protesting a recent South African law that would force them to register as foreigners in the country. Two years of mass meetings and rallies led up to this event at which Gandhi and his followers broke the law by burning their registration papers. No one had any idea that these actions marked the beginning of a movement that would change the world. In South Africa Gandhi defined the philosophy and developed the tactics he would use over the next forty years to lead the unarmed people of India in a nonviolent uprising against the British Empire. Using nothing but their bodies, their intelligence, and their wills, these Indian laborers, housewives, shopkeepers, and students challenged a well-armed military force that had occupied their country for three hundred years. The world had never seen anything like it.

Gandhi was not the first leader to use nonviolent

methods to challenge injustice, but he developed new strategies involving tens of thousands of people in mass actions and demonstrated the power of nonviolence on a scale never seen before. Gandhi became the father of modern nonviolent resistance, which combined truth, love, and the refusal to cause harm into a force that could overcome the most brutal violence and oppression.

The Indian Independence Movement inspired similar actions all over the world. From sunny grape fields in California to the chilly streets of Prague, on buses and in prisons, in groups of thousands or standing alone, struggling people all over the world have chosen to follow the way of Gandhi. Some were directly inspired by his words and deeds, others came to embrace nonviolent resistance on a different path. All made the same commitment: to fight injustice without sacrificing their own humanity.

Facing daunting obstacles, these people accomplished seemingly impossible things. They stood up to armies of soldiers with guns and tanks, secret police who tortured and killed, dictatorships, unjust laws, gangs of thugs, and sometimes even the majority of their country's citizens, who were fearful of the change they sought. They faced these obstacles without resorting to violence. And most amazingly, they sometimes won.

Told here are some of their stories. But only some. We have selected a group of people who represent the diverse, global nature of nonviolent resistance and its range of causes, who engaged in direct action, and who lived the Gandhian ideals of self-sacrifice and overcoming hate with love. There are many people who aren't in this book, and we encourage readers to seek out these other stories of resistance.

BE THE CHANGE YOU WANT TO SEE IN THE WORLD. MOHANDAS GANDHI

In relating the stories of nonviolent resisters, it is important to be truthful. The accounts in this book are about real people who faced real danger. They all had both strengths and weaknesses, they made mistakes, and they weren't always successful. What matters most is that these ordinary people had the courage to take a stand without resorting to violence or hate. This is particularly important, because the story of nonviolent resistance doesn't end with the people in this book.

This is not a history book, relating only things that happened in the past. Nonviolent resistance is a living, breathing, changing tradition. It is going on right now, in places across the globe, wherever people are trying to make the world a better place. New ideas and new strategies are being invented all the time, and children are being born who will use nonviolence to change the world again.

—*Anne Sibley O'Brien and Perry Edmond O'Brien*

IF WE ARE TO TEACH REAL PEACE IN THIS WORLD, AND IF WE ARE TO CARRY ON A REAL WAR AGAINST WAR, WE SHALL HAVE TO BEGIN WITH THE CHILDREN.

MOHANDAS GANDHI

1908

JOHANNESBURG, SOUTH AFRICA

THE CROWD PRESSED into the city square. Some three thousand Indian men had gathered—Muslim, Hindu, and Christian. Some wore English-style suits and hats; others were dressed in traditional Indian tunics and turbans or rectangular caps. They had come to break a law.

At the front of the crowd, a large three-legged pot stood on a platform. A stack of nearly two thousand papers, registration certificates and licenses that the South African government required Indian citizens to carry, was placed in the pot. Wax was poured over the papers and the stack was set alight. An enormous cheer rose with the flames and smoke as the papers burned. The men yelled and whistled and threw hats into the air. A group of Chinese men then mounted the platform. Their certificates were added to the fire.

The shouting was so loud that it was a long time

before the leaders on the platform could address the crowd. When they finally could be heard, one of the men to give a speech was an Indian lawyer named Mohandas Gandhi.

The campaign of the South African Indians against unfair laws that treated them differently from white citizens had begun nearly two years before. But this was the first action in which a mass of people deliberately broke the law. A reporter from a British paper compared the action to the Boston Tea Party.

PLEASE DO NOT LOOK TO MY LIFE, BUT TAKE ME EVEN AS A LAMPPOST ON THE ROAD. MOHANDAS GANDHI

MOHANDAS KARAMCHAND GANDHI was born to a Hindu family in India in 1869. At the time, Britain ruled over India. As a young boy Gandhi had a model of courage and independence in his father, who dared to challenge an insulting remark made by a British political agent about an Indian prince. The agent was furious and had Gandhi's father arrested, but he eventually dropped the charges, and the two became friends.

Gandhi's mother had the deepest influence on the young boy through her tenderness. Though she could seem strict because she held such high standards for her children's behavior, one of the standards of her moral code was kindness and compassion. Every morning there were twenty or thirty desperately poor people waiting at the gate to the Gandhi household, knowing they would be given money or food.

In grade school Gandhi was introduced to Indian poetry. One verse in particular stayed with him his whole life. The poem spoke of the virtue of using love to overcome injustice. "If a man gives you a drink of water and you give him a drink in return, that is nothing," the verse said. "Real beauty consists in doing good against evil." Gandhi was also influenced by the philosophy of nonviolence or *ahimsa*, practiced by the many followers of the Jain religion who lived in his community.

As a young man Gandhi traveled to London to study

law. There he discovered the words of Jesus in the Sermon on the Mount, which said, "Love your enemies and pray for them that persecute you." Gandhi also reread a Hindu scripture, the Bhagavad Gita, to which he had been introduced as a boy. Finally he read work by the Russian writer Leo Tolstoy, which was full of passionate sympathy for peasants who were treated unjustly.

The young Indian lawyer who arrived in South Africa in 1893 was a shy and soft-spoken man who had no dreams of becoming a leader of any kind. He was the model of a perfect British gentleman, speaking impeccable English, dressed in English clothing, committed to the values of British law and empire.

Soon after his arrival in South Africa, he had an experience that set the course of his life in a new direction. He was traveling by train on a first-class ticket when a white passenger objected to sharing the coach with a dark-skinned occupant. The train conductor ordered Gandhi to the third-class car. When he refused he was thrown off the train at the next station, where he spent the night outside, shivering in the cold. The next day Gandhi took a horse-drawn coach. Once again he was told to give up his seat. When Gandhi continued to sit there, the driver began to beat him until a white passenger protested.

These personal experiences of injustice shocked the young lawyer. Though he had intended to return to India, he was persuaded to remain and practice law among his countrymen in Johannesburg, working to improve the conditions of their lives. Gandhi helped form an association of Indian citizens and began to speak out.

In 1906 the South African government passed the Asiatic Registration Act. All Asian residents were required to register and be fingerprinted. No white citizens had to register. The Indian community was outraged; fingerprinting was for criminals.

NONVIOLENCE IS AN INTENSELY ACTIVE FORCE WHEN PROPERLY UNDERSTOOD AND USED. MOHANDAS GANDHI

At a mass meeting on September 11, 1906, Gandhi made his first call for a nonviolent response. For a number of years he had been reflecting on the potential for powerful resistance using nonviolent means. He knew of examples of protests and boycotts in Ireland, India, and South Africa and had kept track of the massive nonviolent uprisings of Russian citizens in 1905.

Though in his 1906 speech he used the term "passive resistance," he soon challenged the use of it to describe his work. Passive resistance suggested weakness or not doing anything. Also, though nonviolent, such resistance could be motivated by hate or anger.

Gandhi had a different vision. He sought to replace violence with love, not just in his actions, but in his mind and heart as well. He imagined nonviolent *action* with the goal not of beating opponents, but of winning them over.

Within two years he found an Indian name for his idea—*satyagraha*. It combined the word for truth, *satya*, with the word *agraha*, for firmness or force. He believed that refusing to harbor violence of any kind was a choice that came out of strength, not weakness. And he saw the possibility that it could be extraordinarily powerful. By *satyagraha* Gandhi meant the strength of active nonviolent resistance to injustice.

The mass burning of registration papers in August 1908 was one of many acts of resistance led by Gandhi in South Africa, where he had a chance to experiment with his new ideas. Gandhi taught that if a law was unjust and caused harm, a moral person had a responsibility to resist it. Laws could be resisted by noncooperation: refusing to go along with them, such as refusing to be fingerprinted. "Noncooperation with evil is as much a duty as is cooperation with good," Gandhi said. Laws could also be resisted by civil disobedience, which means breaking a law in order to change it. When the Indians burned their registration cards, they were practicing civil disobedience.

The more Gandhi supported the cause of Indian workers in South Africa, the more he came to identify with them. His closest supporters lived with him in a separate religious community, or ashram. There everyone shared the physical work equally.

For seven years Gandhi and his followers used noncooperation and civil disobedience to protest the mistreatment of Indians in South Africa. The Indian protesters were beaten, arrested, jailed, and some were even shot, but they refused to give up or to resort to violence. Finally, in 1914, the Minister of the Interior, General J.C. Smuts, was forced to negotiate an agreement with Gandhi, giving in to many of his demands. The Indians' Relief Act was passed, overturning some of the most restrictive laws. Gandhi's campaign on behalf of Indians in South Africa had succeeded.

In 1915 he took his message and his methods home to India. The man who returned to his homeland was dressed not in the clothes of an English gentleman, but in the draped cloth of the poor.

For more than thirty years, Gandhi organized nonviolent resistance against the British occupation of India. Throughout those years he also worked tirelessly to bring together different groups of Indians, especially Hindus and Muslims. All these actions were guided by his absolute commitment to a loving nonviolence, *ahimsa,* which means never causing harm.

In his later years Gandhi was an odd figure, a little man in a loincloth whose personal possessions became simpler each year. At the ashram he and his followers spent hours in prayer and meditation, and an hour or two each day spinning cotton thread. By his example he hoped to encourage Indians to make their own cloth instead of depending on fabric imported from England.

Gandhi was a strict vegetarian and also tried experimental diets of very limited foods that were not always good for his health. He believed in self-sacrifice in all aspects of life, and in the expectation of suffering in the pursuit of what was right. When he could think of no other action, he announced a personal fast, going without food as a means of calling attention to injustice. To millions of Indians he was known as the Mahatma, or "Great One."

The Great Salt March of 1930 was perhaps his most famous action. At the time the British had a tax on salt. Though it was a free natural resource, abundantly available along India's coast, the British wanted to control salt. They outlawed the collection and distribution anywhere but at official salt depots, where it was taxed. Gandhi saw the salt tax as a cruel injustice to the poorest people, who had to pay for something that should have been free, like the air and the water. He also saw it as a perfect example of the evil of a foreign government controlling the lives of people whose land they had occupied. He decided to defy the law.

He set out on March 12, 1930, with seventy-eight followers, marching for twenty-five days to the sea. Along the way he passed through villages where he spoke out against the salt tax. More and more people joined the march. By the time they reached the coast on April 5, more than fifty thousand had gathered, and the eyes of India, the British government, and the world were on Gandhi. The following morning he reached down and scooped up a handful of salt from the shore.

Gandhi was arrested a month later. That year, more than sixty thousand Indians were put in jail for following his example. The action caused political groups all over India to unite in the struggle for independence and put enormous pressure on the British. By 1931 Gandhi was involved in negotiations with the occupation government.

In 1946 India achieved independence from England. But Gandhi didn't feel triumphant at the victory, because at the same time India became independent, it was divided. A law called the Partition, enacted in 1947, separated India's Muslims from its Hindus, creating the new country of Pakistan for Muslims. Gandhi was heartbroken. All the work he had done to heal the divisions between Muslims and Hindus seemed to have failed.

Gandhi was assassinated in 1948 by a Hindu man who hated his attempts to bring Hindus and Muslims together. At the time of his death the Mahatma was known around the world. He was a leader who, half a century after his death, continues to inspire other leaders in every corner of the globe. Some walk Gandhi's path in their vision of peacemaking and their ability to call others to peace. Others follow in his footsteps as they respond to the needs of the poor. Still others have studied the ideas of community he attempted to model on his ashrams.

There are those who have continued to experiment with active nonviolent strategies of resistance to evil, whether or not they directly followed Gandhi.

By his words, his actions, and his example, Mahatma Gandhi left the world a new teaching: to oppose injustice with the force of unrelenting truth and a nonviolent spirit, overcoming hate with love, while being willing to sacrifice oneself for the cause. He demonstrated at an entirely new level the power and possibility of individual and mass nonviolent resistance, a legacy that people all over the world continue to explore.

MOHANDAS GANDHI, 1869–1948

Gandhi's first acts of nonviolent resistance took place in South Africa, not in his homeland of India, because he had moved there to serve the Indian community as a lawyer. South Africa is home to a large number of Indians who are descendants of workers brought from India by the British for labor on sugar plantations and in mines as early as 1860.

Living in South Africa and later India, Gandhi worked side by side with Muslims, Hindus, and people from a variety of other religions. Both countries are home to people of many different religious traditions, including followers of three of the world's largest faiths: Christianity, Islam, and Hinduism. Hinduism is the oldest religion in the world and is practiced mainly in India. It is a broad term that covers many different beliefs and spiritual practices, including yoga. Many Hindus believe in more than one god.

Islam is the world's second-largest religion. People who practice Islam are called Muslims. Like Christians and Jews, Muslims believe in one god. Mosques are the places where Muslims go to pray and worship God, whom they call Allah.

During most of Gandhi's life, India was ruled by the British Empire. An empire is a country that takes over and controls other countries. When an empire invades another country and stays there, it is called an occupation. Many nonviolent movements have been aimed at ending occupations.

1947

RURAL VIETNAM

ONE MORNING on a remote hilltop path in the Vietnamese countryside, a young Buddhist monk encountered a French soldier. The monk's name was Thich Nhat Hanh, and he had every reason to be afraid of the soldier he saw running toward him.

France had ruled Vietnam for years, but now the people were rising up, leading to a bloody confrontation with the French army. Not even monks were safe from this violence. The French had attacked monasteries and even executed monks, many of whom they claimed had joined the resistance. Despite his fear, Thich Nhat Hanh decided not to run away. He approached the young soldier. As it turned out, the Frenchman only wanted to talk.

The soldier told Thich Nhat Hanh that he and his squad had recently been ordered to search a temple for weapons. Instead of finding guns, they came upon fifty monks sitting together in perfect silence. The monks were meditating and didn't even respond to the sudden intrusion. The French soldiers were so impressed by this *courage that they went outside and waited under a tree until the monks had finished meditating. When someone finally came out to see what they wanted, the squad just thanked him and left.*

Now the young French soldier was beginning to question the war, and he wanted to know all about Buddhism. This conversation blossomed into a friendship, and soon the soldier was visiting Thich Nhat Hanh's temple for vegetarian meals and meditation training.

THE PRACTICE OF PEACE AND RECONCILIATION IS ONE OF THE MOST VITAL AND ARTISTIC OF HUMAN ACTIONS. THICH NHAT HANH

THICH NHAT HANH'S relationship with the French soldier reinforced a basic Buddhist teaching: all people are essentially good and want to be free of suffering. Like Gandhi, Buddhists believe that this basic human goodness is much more important than any political or religious affiliation. To find goodness in others we must have the courage to approach people with a calm and compassionate heart. Writing on this subject, Thich Nhat Hanh later said, "If in our daily life we can smile, if we can be peaceful and happy, not only we, but everyone will profit from it. This is the most basic kind of peace work."

Soon after his soldier friend returned to France, Thich Nhat Hanh completed his training as a monk. Now that he had learned to discover his own inner peace, he set out to make peace in the world. In 1960 Thich Nhat Hanh moved to Saigon to join a growing movement of younger monks who wanted Buddhism to better serve the people. By then the French had left Vietnam, but now the country was divided by a terrible civil war. The North wanted to unite Vietnam under communist rule, while the South was trying to maintain an equally oppressive regime supported by the United States. The Vietnam War was devastating the country, as bombs and napalm fell from the sky and great armies clashed in the jungle. Millions of people were killed, including Thich Nhat Hanh's brother, and many more were forced from their homes.

Both the North and the South wanted the monks to take a side in the war. Thich Nhat Hanh refused. Despite threats from both governments, he remained deeply committed to nonviolent action. In 1964 Thich Nhat Hanh started the School of Youth for Social Service, a Buddhist student organization that rebuilt villages, opened schools and medical centers, and found new homes for people whose communities had been destroyed. Thousands of students joined the school, traveling fearlessly into war zones to rebuild their country and help their fellow citizens.

Many villagers were suspicious of this outside help because of all they had suffered. Thich Nhat Hanh taught students how to earn people's trust by becoming part of the community. Most importantly Thich Nhat Hanh and his students taught villagers how to help themselves.

Thich Nhat Hanh did this work even as the South Vietnamese government started making laws that oppressed Buddhists. He and thousands of other monks marched in protest against these laws. Some monks set themselves on fire to show that they would endure even the worst suffering to protect their religion. As the war continued, Thich Nhat Hanh left his homeland to travel the world and raise awareness of the horrors of the Vietnam War. He spoke with political and religious leaders and at churches and universities, always advocating a peaceful solution to the conflict. For refusing to take sides in the war, Thich Nhat Hanh was exiled from his homeland in 1967. He found a home in France. Even after the war ended in 1975, he was not allowed to return.

Though in exile, Thich Nhat Hanh has never stopped working for world peace while teaching others to find their own inner peace. Recently he has been allowed to visit Vietnam and has made several trips there with large delegations of monks and others practicing Buddhism. He spends most of his time in a retreat called Plum Village in France, the homeland of the young soldier he befriended more than half a century ago.

IF IN OUR DAILY LIFE WE CAN SMILE, IF WE CAN BE PEACEFUL AND HAPPY, NOT ONLY WE, BUT EVERYONE, WILL PROFIT FROM IT. THIS IS THE MOST BASIC KIND OF PEACE WORK. THICH NHAT HANH

THICH NHAT HANH. 1926-

Buddhism is one of the world's major religions. Unlike followers of other religions, most Buddhists don't worship a god or gods, but focus on living a balanced life, avoiding extremes in all things and showing respect for all forms of life. Buddhist monks are those who have completely devoted themselves to religious life. Communities of monks live together in monasteries. Most monks shave their heads, wear robes, and lead very simple lives of meditation, work, and study. Meditation is a key method of Buddhist practice. The goal of meditation is to calm the mind and become truly aware of the world.

Thich Nhat Hanh grew up in a divided Vietnam. The northern part of the country was ruled by a communist regime. A regime is a particular government or set of rules. Communism is a form of government based on the ideal of common ownership, where everyone shares everything. The southern half of Vietnam was anticommunist, like the United States. When the North and South began fighting, the United States sided with the South. This conflict was called the Vietnam War, which lasted fifteen years and resulted in millions of deaths.

1955

MONTGOMERY, ALABAMA, USA

IN THE DECEMBER DUSK, *the city bus rolled to a stop. Black and white workers on their way home filed through the bus doors—whites through the front, blacks through the back. One white man was left standing. The driver ordered the four black riders in the front of the "colored" section to give up their seats so white people could sit down.*

Three of them stood up. The fourth, a middle-aged woman named Rosa Parks, remained in her seat.

"Are you going to stand up?" the bus driver demanded, his tone threatening. In 1955 in Montgomery, Alabama, the bus drivers carried pistols.

Gentle, soft-spoken Rosa Parks replied, "No."

ROSA PARKS began life as Rosa McCauley. She was a quiet, shy child. Often sick with tonsillitis, she didn't get to play a lot with other children. Her family had little money but plenty of pride. At home and in the church she attended regularly, Parks was taught that she should never allow herself to be mistreated.

Mistreatment was a daily experience for black Americans in the time of segregation. This system kept African Americans from voting, holding certain jobs, and using public services like restaurants, water fountains, and front-of-the-bus seats that were reserved for whites.

There was a time in Parks's young life when bands of white men, armed with torches and guns, rode on horseback through the streets of her town of Pine Level, Alabama. They wore white robes with pointed hoods and were called the Ku Klux Klan. The KKK threatened black residents, set fire to black churches, and even killed people. At night Parks's grandfather slept in a rocking chair with a shotgun in his lap, ready to defend his family. Though gentle, Parks had a fierce heart, so she curled up on the floor beside him. "I remember thinking that whatever happened, I wanted to see it," she said. "I wanted to see him shoot that gun."

Rosa Parks is often portrayed as a meek, unassuming woman. As a member of the National Association for the Advancement of Colored People (NAACP) however, she was trained as an activist. In the summer of 1955, she attended Highlander Folk School where she learned about strategies to end segregation, including the nonviolent tactics Mohandas Gandhi had recently used to gain India's independence. This education strengthened her resolve to resist injustice. Four months later she got on a bus one evening and made the decision to stand up for herself by staying seated. She's often described as having been too tired to give up her seat. "The only tired I was, was tired of giving in," she said.

Keeping her seat took considerable courage, because it wasn't the first time Rosa Parks had been mistreated by the same bus driver, James Blake. He was a vicious man who often insulted and threatened black passengers. Twelve years before, he had been driving a bus so crowded that there was no room to get on in the back. When Parks got on in the front, he told her to go to the back. She refused. He ordered her off his bus. She complied, feeling ashamed. From that day on she vowed to never get on a bus that he was driving. For twelve years she had avoided James Blake. But on the night of December 1, 1955, Parks didn't notice who the bus driver was until he ordered her to move.

She wasn't the first person to refuse to give up her seat. Three other black women in Montgomery did the same thing that year, as a number of others had done in years before. When Rosa Parks was arrested, though, the civil rights movement leaders saw an opportunity. The soft-spoken, law-abiding seamstress was the perfect person to demonstrate the unfairness of segregation.

> # I HAD NO IDEA THAT HISTORY WAS BEING MADE. I WAS JUST TIRED OF GIVING IN. ROSA PARKS

By the date of her trial four days later, a group of activists had printed fliers, made contacts, and organized the entire black community to begin the Montgomery Bus Boycott. Instead of taking the bus, black citizens walked to work or caught rides with the fleet of black-owned taxicabs and carpools that were mobilized. For one year and one month, in hot sun, fierce wind, or pelting rain, the seventeen thousand black citizens of Montgomery used the power of their feet to try to overturn an unfair system.

In December 1956 the law was changed. The people of Montgomery, black and white, could sit in any seat on any bus. It was actually another court case, not the boycott, which resulted in the new law. But it was Parks's famous action that brought the world's attention to the black struggle for equality. This led to the end of other kinds of segregation. Rosa Parks's refusal to be mistreated was like a match lighting a fire to the civil rights movement. "At the time I was arrested I had no idea it would turn into this," she said later. "It was just a day like any other day. The only thing that made it significant was that the masses of the people joined in."

Though she was familiar with Gandhi's tactics, Rosa Parks did not take the action she did to follow his example. She was clear that she did not always feel nonviolent in her heart. Sitting there on the bus, she thought of her grandfather, sitting in his rocking chair with the shotgun across his lap.

The strategy she chose was nonviolent resistance. Like Gandhi, Rosa Parks demonstrated that the force of nonviolence could be more powerful than any weapon. Her refusal to give up her bus seat became the most famous example of noncooperation in America.

AS LONG AS PEOPLE USE TACTICS TO OPPRESS OR RESTRICT OTHER PEOPLE FROM BEING FREE, THERE IS WORK TO BE DONE. ROSA PARKS

ROSA PARKS. 1913-2005

When Rosa Parks was growing up in the southern United States, segregation was enforced by laws that gave rights to whites but denied them to blacks. This institutionalized injustice wasn't enough for groups like the Ku Klux Klan, America's largest racist organization. The KKK used intimidation, terrorism, and murder to prevent blacks from being treated as equals with whites.

Segregation was challenged by the civil rights movement, a struggle to end discrimination against blacks and other minorities. One of the first decisions against segregation came in 1954, when the US Supreme Court ruled that segregated schools were illegal.

The National Association for the Advancement of Colored People, or NAACP, was a key organization in the civil rights movement. Boycotts were one strategy that the NAACP used to resist injustice. During boycotts, people refused to support institutions or companies that engaged in racist business practices. In Montgomery people refused to ride the bus. Fliers with instructions in nonviolence were distributed to the walkers: "If cursed, do not curse back. If pushed, do not push back."

Rosa Parks's action and the community's response also provided the opportunity for Dr. Martin Luther King, Jr., to emerge as a leader. Serving as a pastor of a local church, King was thrust into a prominent leadership role for the first time by the Montgomery Bus Boycott. The success of the boycott caused King to be recognized across the country as a leader of the civil rights movement.

CAPE TOWN, SOUTH AFRICA

ROBBEN ISLAND, *a wild, rocky outpost seven miles off the coast, was a place of banishment. Nelson Mandela arrived there in the dark belly of a boat, chained to three other men.*

"This is the island! Here you will die!" white prison guards yelled at the four men as they stepped off the boat. They commanded them to jog between lines of armed guards to the prison gatehouse. Mandela knew this moment was crucial. The job of the guards was to break their spirit. As the jailers screamed at them, he and the others kept their pace slow.

The guards were astonished. They threatened to kill the men if they did not move faster. Mandela replied, "You have your duty, and we have ours," and walked with measured dignity to the gates.

He spent the next twenty-seven years in prison.

NELSON MANDELA had been born into a royal household in the Thembu clan of the Xhosa nation in South Africa. As a young boy he spent his days outside, herding goats, cattle, horses, and sheep, and stick fighting with the other boys. His father died when Mandela was nine, and the boy was sent to live with the Thembu chief, who raised him to be an advisor to the king. But he left home and ended up in Johannesburg. It was his work there as a lawyer that opened his eyes to the injustices that black South Africans were suffering.

At that time the nation of South Africa was ruled by a brutal system called apartheid, which means "apartness." Though there were many fewer white South Africans than black, the white minority held complete power and control over the country. The black majority could not even

TO MAKE PEACE WITH AN ENEMY ONE MUST WORK WITH THAT ENEMY, AND THAT ENEMY BECOMES ONE'S PARTNER. NELSON MANDELA

vote. Secret police raids, army tanks and guns, house arrest, imprisonment, torture, and killings were used to keep the system in place.

Mandela and his compatriots were members of the African National Congress (ANC), which called for "one man, one vote" and a democratic nation for all races. The ANC started as an organization dedicated to nonviolence. Their 1952 Defiance Campaign had been modeled on Gandhi's methods. However, Nelson Mandela and some other members were not pacifists. Convinced that the government's violence would never change without armed resistance, the fiery lawyer had helped form a military group to train soldiers to fight back. For these actions he was sentenced to life imprisonment on Robben Island.

At the prison the leaders of the anti-apartheid movement—black, Indian and "colored," or mixed race—were housed together in one section. At first they spent their days breaking rocks into gravel. Then for thirteen years they mined limestone from a quarry with picks and shovels. They were fed cold corn porridge. They slept in individual cells, on mats on cement floors, surrounded by thick stone walls. Many of the prisoners had life sentences.

Mandela believed he would be freed one day. He knew that his challenge was to survive in both body and spirit, to emerge from prison whole. He and the other leaders began a campaign to improve their conditions. They decided that the most effective way to resist was to adopt completely nonviolent strategies. They organized strikes, refusing to eat or slowing down their work. They treated their guards with respect and when possible befriended them, but they refused to be bullied. At first they demanded long pants instead of the shorts they were given, which only boys wore. Over many years they won better food, more blankets, and the chance to have more visitors, to write letters, to study, to receive books.

Meanwhile they transformed the prison into a place of learning. Stolen newspapers, read in secret by one person, were copied on tiny scraps of paper and passed around. As one man pushed a rock-filled wheelbarrow in the quarry, another walked beside him, telling him what he knew of science or mathematics or philosophy. When books and studies were finally allowed, everything learned was shared with others. Group debates might go on for thirty or forty days, working out differences among the men and visions of how the country should be run.

In 1982 Mandela and several other leaders were transferred to another prison where the government hoped to have more control over them. The officials of the regime wanted to isolate these anti-apartheid champions from the other prisoners at Robben Island, and they also wanted to create opportunities for secret negotiations with them.

Mandela and his colleagues took their struggle for dignity with them. "The campaign to improve conditions in prison was part of the apartheid struggle," Mandela wrote in his autobiography. "We fought injustice wherever we found it, no matter how large, or how small, and we fought injustice to preserve our own humanity."

In 1990 under intense pressure from within South Africa and from countries around the world, the government released Nelson Mandela from prison. He spent the next four years in talks, negotiating the nonviolent transfer of power. On April 27, 1994, the entire country participated in an election. The seventy-five-year-old Mandela and his fellow black South Africans voted for the first time in their lives. Nelson Mandela was elected president. The ideas that had been chipped out of the hard prison years became the basis for the government of the new South Africa.

WE FOUGHT INJUSTICE WHEREVER WE FOUND IT, NO MATTER HOW LARGE, OR HOW SMALL, AND WE FOUGHT INJUSTICE TO PRESERVE OUR OWN HUMANITY. NELSON MANDELA

NELSON MANDELA. 1918–

Nelson Mandela lived in South Africa during apartheid, a system of racial oppression even more brutal than American segregation. Apartheid was designed as a method for the white minority, about one-fifth of the South African population, to control the black majority, about four-fifths of the population.

Under a 1950 law, all South African people were classified by race into one of three categories: Bantu (black African), white, and Colored, which was the term for anyone of mixed race. Indians were considered Colored until a fourth category was added for Asians.

Under apartheid black South Africans were divided into tribes or ethnic groups, forcibly removed from their homes and sent to live in "homelands," poverty-stricken areas with none of the services that whites enjoyed. They were made citizens of one of the homelands and not of the nation of South Africa.

Control of eighty percent of the land passed into the hands of white owners. Residents of black homelands couldn't travel without a passport in South Africa, their own country. In addition, their lives were severely restricted by a series of laws that separated the races in every way imaginable—laws that were brutally enforced.

Resistance to apartheid took many forms. While some South Africans came to believe that only violent resistance could end apartheid, others were committed pacifists who insisted on only nonviolent resistance. A pacifist is someone who, like Gandhi, refuses to use violence for any reason. In fact, one famous South African pacifist was Gandhi's second son, Manilal, who was a member of the African National Congress.

1963

BIRMINGHAM, ALABAMA, USA

THE STREETS WERE FULL *of children. In groups of fifty, lines of singing young black students, from elementary school to college age, poured out of the Sixteenth Street Baptist Church.*

The jails were full of children, too. More than six hundred had been arrested in the march the day before. Since there was no place to put anyone else, Sheriff "Bull" Connor ordered his police force to break up the crowds instead of arresting them.

As the young protestors came into the street, they were met by a wall of white police officers, helmeted and armed with fire hoses. The force of the water knocked children off their feet. One young girl tumbled down the street in the fierce blast from a hose. Still the marchers streamed out of the church, more than a thousand in all. The police brought out K-9 units. Snarling German Shep-

herds strained on the ends of their leashes. Three teenage boys were bitten by the dogs. Still the marchers held their ground, five hundred of them struggling to re-form their lines in the chaos of water and barking dogs and screaming, fleeing people.

Amidst the demonstrators, the onlookers, and the police, there were photographers and cameramen, shooting live footage of the confrontation. That night families gathered in living rooms all over America saw the scenes on the evening news.

In 1963 Birmingham was known for its violence against black citizens. There had been so many bombings—more than fifty—of black homes and churches that some people called the city "Bombingham." It was also known as a city of rigid segregation. In the downtown shopping area, many shops had signs that said, "Whites only." Blacks couldn't use the dressing rooms in clothing stores. They couldn't sit down at a lunch counter to order a sandwich.

IN APRIL 1963 Dr. Martin Luther King, Jr., and his associates arrived in Birmingham at the invitation of local leaders. King was powerfully influenced by the work and writings of Gandhi, whom he'd begun reading more than a decade earlier. Another leader of the civil rights movement, James Farmer, had been using Gandhi's tactics in organizing student sit-ins in Nashville, Tennessee. Now King planned to use the same approach in Birmingham.

To persuade store owners to change their unfair treatment, the black community organized a boycott of downtown businesses. In response the city government pressured a judge to declare boycotts, marches, and sit-ins illegal.

That month was a difficult time for the civil rights movement. Even among those who were following him, many disagreed with King's approach in Birmingham. Not only the white community but the majority of the city's black ministers did not support his actions. King and the campaign were criticized in national magazines and newspapers. Fewer and fewer people were coming out for the demonstrations. The movement also knew that anyone who dared to march risked being jailed for long sentences. The campaign had paid so much to bail people out of jail that they had nearly run out of money. In the midst of all this turmoil, King and his wife also had a new baby at home.

For all these reasons many of King's associates urged him not to march. But, King argued, if the city succeeded in stopping the protests, the segregationists would win. He didn't know how things would work out, but he decided that he had to defy the ruling, even if he did it alone.

On April 12 the march was held, fifty-two people were arrested, and King was thrown into solitary confinement in the Birmingham jail. While in jail King read a story in a newspaper smuggled in by his lawyer. Eight white ministers had made a statement about King's actions in Birmingham. Though these ministers were actually in favor of ending segregation, they felt that King was demanding too much too fast. The ministers said he should sit down and talk instead of demonstrating and marching.

WE SHALL MEET YOUR PHYSICAL FORCE WITH SOUL FORCE. DR. MARTIN LUTHER KING, JR.

King started making notes in the margins of the newspaper. The movement was waiting for instructions about what to do next. But when his lawyer visited again, King only wanted to discuss the letter he was composing. He secretly slipped his notes through the bars of his cell and asked his lawyer to get the message out to the public.

The letter King wrote in jail was a passionate response

from a minister to the eight ministers who had criticized him. He explained why he and his followers couldn't be patient anymore. He wrote about beatings and lynchings, about name-calling and disrespect. He wrote about having to explain to his little daughter why she wasn't allowed into the amusement park, and to his young son how some white people could be so mean. He wrote about unjust laws and why it was necessary to challenge them: "One who breaks an unjust law must do so openly, lovingly, and with a willingness to accept the penalty. I submit that an individual who breaks a law that conscience tells him is unjust, and who willingly accepts the penalty of imprisonment in order to arouse the conscience of the community over its injustice, is in reality expressing the highest respect for law."

When the letter was typed and distributed, there was absolutely no response. None of the ministers it was addressed to made any comment. The press was not interested in something written by a troublemaker preacher who couldn't stay out of jail.

On May 3 Bull Connor turned his fire hoses and police dogs on the children. The nation and the world were shocked at the violence against young citizens who had done nothing but gather for a nonviolent demonstration. Under national pressure the Birmingham businessmen agreed to open the lunch counters and dressing rooms, the

ONE WHO BREAKS AN UNJUST LAW MUST DO SO OPENLY, LOVINGLY, AND WITH A WILLINGNESS TO ACCEPT THE PENALTY. DR. MARTIN LUTHER KING, JR.

restrooms and water fountains, to nonwhite people. Within a month newspapers all over the country began to print the "Letter from Birmingham Jail." Soon it was a famous document, and the work of Dr. Martin Luther King, Jr., and the American civil rights movement became known around the world, inspiring those struggling for freedom everywhere.

"We shall match your capacity to inflict suffering with our capacity to endure suffering," King wrote in an earlier sermon composed in another jail. "We shall meet your physical force with soul force. Do to us what you will, and we shall continue to love you. . . . But be assured that we will wear you down by our capacity to suffer. One day we shall win freedom, but not only for ourselves. We shall so appeal to your heart and conscience that we shall win you in the process, and our victory will be a double victory."

DR. MARTIN LUTHER KING, JR. 1929–1968

In Birmingham, Alabama, in 1963 black citizens did not have the law on their side. In addition to being denied voting, access to equal education, and other rights, African Americans across the South were sometimes at the mercy of white citizens who took the law into their own hands. One terrible practice of the time was lynching, in which people were murdered by being hanged from trees. Though sometimes accused of having committed crimes, these victims were not given trials, but were convicted by violent lynch mobs who punished them with death. Lynching was also used to intimidate the black population so that people would be afraid to fight against injustices.

African Americans couldn't count on the courts to protect them from such violence, and the practices that made them second-class citizens were enforced by law. But across the nation, change had slowly been coming. In 1946 the Supreme Court had declared that there could be no segregated seating on buses traveling between states. In 1948 President Harry Truman had ordered all branches of the military to be integrated. In 1954 the Supreme Court had declared that segregated schools were illegal, and in 1956 Alabama's segregated seating on buses had been outlawed, again by the Supreme Court. Bit by bit, the foundation of laws that upheld segregation had been chipped away.

Throughout the South, however, governors and mayors, police chiefs and judges were determined to defend their old way of life. They refused to obey the Supreme Court rulings. The civil rights leaders knew they also had to apply pressure to the existing laws through civil disobedience. The violent reactions to their civil disobedience, and the refusal of officials to obey the laws of the nation, forced the US government, headed by President John F. Kennedy and his brother, Attorney General Robert F. Kennedy, to take a stand on civil rights.

1965

MOREE, AUSTRALIA

IT WAS A HOT DAY, *and the crowd of white townspeople was furious. Thirty university students had gathered at the gate to the town pool, and they weren't letting anyone in. Except for their leader, the students were white, but they were there on behalf of black Aborigine children, who weren't allowed to use the pool.*

First the crowd shouted insults at the students. No one moved. Then they started to throw eggs and rotten fruit. Some of them spit on the students and threw handfuls of dirt and gravel. Soon the students were covered in filth, but they refused to budge.

By midday the crowd had swelled to almost a thousand people. They began throwing rocks and broken bottles. They punched students, pushed them, knocked them to the ground. Still the students stood at the gate, using their bodies as a living barrier.

The Students for Aboriginal Action had made a simple decision: until black Aboriginal children were allowed into the public pool, no one would swim.

ABORIGINES ARE the indigenous people of Australia, but they were treated as second-class citizens. Denied access to many private and public places, Aborigines were pushed to the margins of society to live in shantytowns. Aborigines couldn't vote, had inadequate legal protection, and were often treated like animals.

The Students for Aboriginal Action were led by Charles Perkins, an Aboriginal man who was no stranger to racism and injustice. He was born in a shantytown called Alice Springs in 1936. When he was six he was taken from his home by a minister who wanted to give Aborigines an English and Christian education. Perkins spent the next ten years in a boardinghouse for Aboriginal children, where he was subjected to beatings and racist insults by those who were supposed to be caring for him. Outside of the boardinghouse, in a white suburb, the attacks and humiliations only got worse.

TODAY WE STRUGGLE FOR THE SOUL OF OUR COUNTRY. CHARLES PERKINS

"You learned from when you were a kid to stay out of the way of whites," he said in an interview. "Our big treat was being taken to the pictures, sneaking in after the movie had started, and leaving before it ended, so that no one would object to us black kids being there."

Charles Perkins never let himself be intimidated by whites. He knew he was as good as any other person. At age fourteen, he found a way to prove it, through the game of soccer. One day he and his friends were challenged to a match by older boys from the state soccer team. Though they had never played before, the bare-footed Aborigines beat the older, uniformed boys 10–0. Perkins went on to join local soccer clubs and became such a great player that he was invited to join a team in England. In Europe he saw that not all black people were subjected to the same abuses as Aborigines in Australia.

Returning home two years later, Perkins began to blaze a new path for Aborigines. He became the first Aboriginal soccer star and the first Aborigine to attend university. It was at Sydney University that Perkins organized concerned white students to form the Students for Aboriginal Action. He served as the group's president. Perkins had been inspired by the Freedom Rides of the US civil rights movement. He decided to take a bus into the Australian outback to expose racism against Aborigines.

By the time the thirty students faced off against a crowd of whites in Moree in 1965, the riders had gained national attention. The newspapers called the Moree crowd "crazed with race-hate," and many Australians were embarrassed: the Australian North was starting to look as bad as the American South. This led to a number of new laws protecting Aborigines, and the Freedom Ride was credited with helping end the "White Australia" policies.

Charles Perkins went on to become an outspoken advocate for Aboriginal rights and was eventually given a government position as the head of the Bureau of Aboriginal Affairs. His stance was simple: "White people have got to recognize this was Aboriginal land before they came here. They haven't been here that long. Accept the history of this country. Then it makes it easy for us to come together, but if we don't accept the history of Australia, we don't come together."

ACCEPT THE HISTORY OF THIS COUNTRY. THEN IT MAKES IT EASY FOR US TO COME TOGETHER. CHARLES PERKINS

CHARLES PERKINS. 1936–2000

Charles Perkins was a child of the "Stolen Generation" in Australia. For more than fifty years, tens of thousands of Aboriginal children were taken from their homes and sent to white institutions or orphanages. This policy was based on the belief that Aborigines were inferior to whites. By forcing Aboriginal children to live in white communities and get Christian educations, the leaders of Australia hoped to slowly destroy Aboriginal culture. This process of trying to absorb one culture into another is called assimilation.

1965

DELANO, CALIFORNIA, USA

AN ENORMOUS FIELD *of grapevines, stretching as far as the eye could see, lay under the hot sun of a California autumn. The grapes were ripe, ready to pick, but the farmworkers were on strike, trying to get better pay. The owners of the vineyard hired other workers, called strikebreakers, to take their places. César Chávez and a group of striking farmworkers gathered at one of the entrances. They hoped to get the strikebreakers to stop work and join the strike. No one would get better pay until everyone refused to work for such low wages.*

As the sun rose and the day heated up, carloads of strikebreakers came through the entrance. A few saw the signs and stopped to join them. But most cars passed the protesters and drove onto the field. The strikebreakers took their places, reaching through the green leaves to pick the grapes. From the entrance, the strikers waved their banners and shouted their slogan, "Huelga! Huelga! Strike! Strike!"

The sound of roaring tractor engines cut through the noise of the crowd. Two huge tractors lumbered toward them out of the fields, driven by foremen of the farm. They came straight toward the strikers, dragging their blades behind them in the dirt. Would they keep going until they ran into the farmworkers? The group stood their ground. Just before hitting them, the tractors suddenly stopped, churning up clouds of brown dust that blew over the strikers. Again and again, for nearly an hour, the tractors backed up and drove at them, until every protester was completely covered with dirt. They refused to budge, continuing to shout to their fellow farmworkers.

Then, from the fields, the protesters saw cars moving toward them. The strikebreakers, who'd been watching the whole episode with growing disgust, had quit work. No more grapes would be picked that day.

AS A YOUNG BOY César Chávez had spent most of his time outdoors on his family's farm, playing with his brother or learning from their father how to work the land. Their mother taught them with sayings and proverbs and particularly emphasized those that offered alternatives to violence. She had deep compassion for poor people and sometimes sent the boys out to look for hungry tramps so she could give them food.

When Chávez was eleven, during the Great Depression, the family lost their farm. They were forced to go on the road, looking for work picking crops. When they could, the children went to school, but Mexican American students were often treated unfairly. Teachers insisted that they speak English and punished them for speaking Spanish, sometimes with beatings. Over three years Chávez attended at least thirty-six different schools in California and Arizona, until he quit eighth grade, when his father was hurt in a car accident. At age thirteen Chávez went to work in the fields full-time to support his family.

In the 1930s, when Chávez was young, the life of a farmworker in California was grim. Out in the fields there were no toilets, no water for drinking or washing, and no rest breaks. Pay was low, and if a farm owner paid even less than he'd promised, there was no law to protect the workers. They stayed in labor camps of flimsy shacks with tin roofs, made their own temporary shelters, or slept in their cars. There were no vacation days, no healthcare or insurance. Farmworkers became sick from picking crops that had been sprayed with toxic chemicals, sometimes even while the workers were in the field.

> # IF WE'RE FULL OF HATRED, WE CAN'T REALLY DO OUR WORK. HATRED SAPS ALL THAT STRENGTH AND ENERGY WE NEED TO PLAN. CÉSAR CHÁVEZ

Little had changed by the early 1960s when, at age thirty-five, Chávez set out to see if he could organize farmworkers. Though Chávez didn't finish eighth grade, he had continued to educate himself by reading. He had read about the work of Gandhi and the astonishing changes brought about in India through organized nonviolence. Chávez had developed organizing skills from his work helping Mexican immigrants register to vote. He was also inspired by the example of his own father, who had quit work many times rather than be mistreated. Imagine what could happen, he thought, if farmworkers gathered together and used the power of their numbers to force the farm owners to improve working conditions.

In 1962 Chávez, Dolores Huerta, and others formed the National Farm Workers Association (NFWA). Their idea was to get farmworkers to join their group, or union. The union would speak for the workers as one voice.

Their first tool was the strike, beginning with the grape farms. If many workers refused to go to work, the owners would lose money until they agreed to talk to the union. The Great Delano Grape Strike began in 1965. It was an action of two unions, the mostly Mexican NFWA and another group that was mostly Filipino workers. The owners of the farms, who had far more money than the union workers, fought hard to stop them. Often the owners had the police and government on their side. The organizers were harassed, threatened, and attacked.

Chávez kept inventing new strategies. The year after the strike began, he led a three-hundred-mile march in California to get attention for the farmworkers. As a result one of the large owners signed an agreement with the union to give their workers better pay and conditions. Nonetheless, there were thousands of other vineyards and farms of other crops where working conditions were still terrible.

The next year Chávez set his eyes on organizing across the entire country. He had been inspired by the Montgomery Bus Boycott. If he could persuade people to stop buying California grapes, that might force the owners to talk. The boycott was the largest that had ever been tried in the United States.

By 1968, two and a half years after the strike had begun, the farmworkers were tired and discouraged. Some of them began to think that the only way to make the owners change was to use violence. Chávez was so committed to nonviolence that, following Gandhi's example of fasting, he decided to engage in a hunger strike.

"I am convinced that the truest act of humanity is to sacrifice ourselves for others in a totally nonviolent struggle for justice," Chávez said. He fasted for twenty-five days, drinking only water, until the strikers pledged to follow nonviolent methods.

Five years after the strike began, the grape growers finally signed contracts with the farmworkers union. But the struggle had just begun. Chávez worked tirelessly for "La Causa," the cause of the farmworkers, until his death at sixty-six. The struggle continues today. Because of César Chávez, the lives of California's and the nation's farmworkers have been changed forever.

CÉSAR CHÁVEZ. 1927–1993

César Chávez grew up during the Great Depression (1929–1939), a time of enormous hardship in the United States. Many Americans had no jobs at all, or got paid very little. Many people lived in poverty, and many had to travel to look for work.

Since the late 1700s, groups of American workers have joined together to form unions, organizations which protect workers' rights and guarantee fair pay and benefits. Because the union represents many workers, it can negotiate with owners. The ability to strike, or refuse to work, is the union's most powerful tool. When a union of workers organizes a strike, they put pressure on an employer to improve conditions in order to get them to go back to work. Strikebreakers, or "scabs," are temporary workers called in to replace strikers.

In 1966 the National Farm Workers Association joined with the Filipino farmworkers of the Agricultural Workers Organizing Committee to form the United Farmworkers of America, or UFW. The UFW is one of the largest labor unions in the United States.

One method Chávez used to gain improved conditions for workers was the hunger strike, a strategy of nonviolent resistance that Gandhi developed as a form of protest and as a way of pressuring his followers to renounce violence.

HOUSTON, TEXAS, USA

THE HEAVYWEIGHT BOXING CHAMPION *of the world sat with twenty-five other young men at an Army induction center. They had all been drafted into the military. One by one, an officer began calling their names. The draftees were supposed to stand up and walk across a yellow line drawn on the floor. Crossing the line meant going to fight in the Vietnam War.*

"Cassius Marcellus Clay," an officer called, but no one answered. Looking directly at the famous boxer, the officer tried again. "Cassius Marcellus Clay!"

Still no reply. The officer warned him that it was a felony to refuse the draft. Again the name was called, and again the champion refused to answer to what he called his "slave name." He had been given another name by the Nation of Islam, which he considered his true name: Muhammad Ali. As a member of the Nation, he was opposed to the war in Vietnam and would not respond to the roll call.

Word spread fast: the most famous fighter in the world was refusing to fight.

Within days the boxing commission took away Ali's boxing license. He lost contracts worth millions of dollars. He faced a five-year prison sentence for draft evasion. Worst of all, Ali was stripped of the championship title he had worked his whole life to earn.

Despite these losses Ali stood by his convictions. He couldn't understand why he should go fight in Vietnam when his own people were being oppressed in America.

"Why should they ask me to put on a uniform and go ten thousand miles from home and drop bombs and bullets on brown people in Vietnam while so-called Negro people in Louisville are treated like dogs and denied simple human rights?" he asked.

ALI WAS A BORN FIGHTER. He started boxing when he was twelve, and by age eighteen he had won ten state and national championships. Ali then went on to the 1960 Rome Olympics, where he won the gold medal for the United States. His victory at the Olympics kicked off an astonishing professional career. He didn't just box well; he changed the way the sport was played. Relying on speed more than strength, Ali would literally dance around opponents. He was known for his colorful poetry, which he would recite to reporters before a fight: "Float like a butterfly, sting like a bee, his hands can't hit what his eyes can't see." Ali also liked to talk himself up. After one fight, he yelled, "I am the greatest thing that ever lived!"

In 1964 Ali shocked the world by defeating Sonny Liston, the reigning heavyweight champion of the world. But the real shock came after the fight.

Addressing reporters, Muhammad Ali announced that he was a member of the controversial Nation of Islam. The Nation was a black nationalist organization founded in Detroit, Michigan, in 1930 on a unique interpretation of the Koran, the Muslims' book of sacred writings. Unlike Dr. Martin Luther King, Jr., the Nation believed that black and white people should be separated. One of the most famous members of the nation was Malcolm X. An important leader in the civil rights movement, Malcolm X was a highly controversial figure in America because he encouraged black people to defend themselves with force against racist violence.

Because of this association, the American press tried to paint Muhammad Ali as a dangerous radical. But Ali resisted the notion that his religion was one of violence.

ISLAM MEANS PEACE. MUHAMMAD ALI

He showed his commitment to living peacefully in many ways. Despite his fame and wealth, he was incredibly kind and giving. Ali was known to give hundred-dollar bills to homeless people he passed on the street. One time Ali heard that a troubled Vietnam veteran was preparing to kill himself by jumping from a building not far from where Ali was staying. Ali drove to the building, got out on the ledge, and began to talk to the young veteran. After a few minutes the two men hugged, and Ali brought the man back inside. After the event Ali paid for new clothes and a place for the veteran to stay.

Muhammad Ali's refusal to be drafted came in the midst of growing opposition to the Vietnam War. Two weeks before his announcement, four hundred thousand people had marched to the United Nations building in New York City to protest the war. One of the antiwar speakers that day was Dr. Martin Luther King, Jr. But despite the unpopularity of the US involvement in Vietnam, the war went on for another eight years.

I HAVE NOTHING TO LOSE BY STANDING UP AND FOLLOWING MY BELIEFS. SO I'LL GO TO JAIL, SO WHAT? WE'VE BEEN IN JAIL FOR 400 YEARS. MUHAMMAD ALI

After refusing to go to Vietnam, Ali was suspended from boxing for three and half years. This was the period during which he reached his physical peak, but he wasn't allowed to test his skill against the best boxers. Finally in 1970 Ali was allowed back in the ring. He went on to regain his title not once, but twice. Ali retired as the first three-time heavyweight champion of the world. Because of the lost years, the world will never know how great "the greatest" could have been.

During this time, public sentiment toward Vietnam had

changed. Ali went from being a controversial figure to being an American hero. In his retirement the great fighter continued to pursue the path of peace. He focused his attention on trying to relieve hunger and poverty all over the world. In 1996 Muhammad Ali returned to the Olympics. Fifty-four years old and crippled from Parkinson's disease, Ali was given the honor of carrying the Olympic torch. On January 12, 2007, the US House of Representatives passed a resolution "to honor Muhammad Ali, global humanitarian, on the occasion of his sixty-fifth birthday."

MUHAMMAD ALI. 1942-

During the Vietnam War the US government instituted a draft to get more soldiers to fight in the war. During the draft young men were forced to serve in the military whether they wanted to or not. It was a felony to refuse to serve, and "draft dodgers" could spend years in jail.

Like Muhammad Ali, thousands of young men resisted the draft. Some burned their draft cards, others challenged the draft in court, and some fled to Canada to avoid serving. Many spent time in jail for refusing to fight.

Opposition to the Vietnam War wasn't limited to draft resistance. Millions of Americans, especially college students, participated in rallies, marches, sit-ins, and other forms of nonviolent protest of the war. One of the most outspoken leaders was Dr. Martin Luther King, Jr., who particularly urged young black men to avoid going to war.

BELFAST, NORTHERN IRELAND

THE RAIN POURED DOWN *in torrents as the Peace People, thousands of them, trudged through the divided city. After decades of violence between paramilitary groups, Belfast was separated by walls into Protestant and Catholic neighborhoods. The Peace People had come to call an end to the violence, and their march was made up of members of both religious groups. They were mostly women, mostly middle-aged, mothers, wives, aunts, and grandmothers. They had been marching for miles past run-down houses, closed shops, and buildings destroyed by bombs. The Peace People sang as they walked, raising their voices above the storm. The singing was to give them courage, for the rain was the least of their concerns. Some Irish saw the Peace People as traitors. The founders of the group, Mairead Corrigan and Betty Williams, had both received death threats.*

As the marchers reached Falls Park, they were met by a group of angry young people. Without warning, the group attacked the marchers, throwing rocks, bricks, and broken bottles. Another group charged the Peace People, hitting and kicking them, pulling their hair and pushing them into the mud. None of the marchers fought back. Instead they huddled together tightly and opened their umbrellas, creating a shield around their group. Many of them were wounded, and they bandaged each other with handkerchiefs. Then they began to walk again, ignoring the hail of rain and the objects thrown at them.

OUR COMMON HUMANITY IS MORE IMPORTANT THAN ALL THE THINGS THAT DIVIDE US. MAIREAD CORRIGAN

1967. BELFAST, NORTHERN IRELAND

LIKE THE CITY of Belfast, all of Northern Ireland was torn by the bitter conflict between Protestants and Catholics. The Protestant majority wanted to remain part of the United Kingdom. Many Catholics, however, wanted a separate and independent country. These divisions went back centuries, to the 1600s when England first occupied Ireland. Though most Irish people wanted to settle this conflict peacefully, in the mid-twentieth century extremists on both sides armed themselves, forming paramilitary groups. The fighting between these groups resulted in a long period of violence and tragedy. The Irish refer to these dark decades, from the 1960s to the 1990s, as "The Troubles."

The war between Protestant and Catholic paramilitary groups had claimed thousands of innocent lives. In some cities there were bombings, shootings, and killings every day. Many people were afraid to leave their homes.

On August 10, 1976, a tragic accident took the lives of three children in the city of Belfast. Anne Maguire was out for a walk with her family. A young driver of a paramilitary getaway car was shot while trying to escape the police after a gun battle. The car spun out of control, hitting the family on the roadside, wounding Anne Maguire and killing her three children.

News of this tragedy created outrage throughout the Belfast community. One of the people most deeply affected was Betty Williams, who had witnessed the accident. She began walking the streets with a petition for peace. In the next few days she was joined by two hundred other women, including Mairead Corrigan, the aunt of the three slain children. The spirit of peace spread like wildfire. Within two weeks, twenty thousand Protestant and Catholic women were marching to demand an end to the violence. Inspired by Gandhi and Dr. Martin Luther King, Jr., Corrigan and Williams believed that nonviolent, mass action was the only way to end violence in Northern Ireland. As Betty Williams would later say, "Nonviolence is the weapon of the strong."

Joined by journalist Ciaran McKeown, Betty Williams and Mairead Corrigan founded the Community of Peace People. In addition to their marches and protests, the Peace People performed civil service to address the root causes of violence. One of the greatest problems of the civil war was that new generations of young people were forced to join the violent groups. Those who didn't want to join were threatened with death. The Peace People helped hundreds of young men escape the paramilitary killers and avoid becoming killers themselves. Another cause of the violence was poverty and lack of equal opportunity. Individuals and organizations all over the world sent money that the Peace People used to reopen factories and feed the poor.

The Peace People's steadfast refusal to engage in violence, even when attacked, eventually won over even some of their fiercest opponents. In fact, in the days following their march through the rain, several of the young people who had thrown rocks at them showed up at their headquarters to apologize. Some even joined the group.

In 1976 Betty Williams and Mairead Corrigan were recognized for their work with the Nobel Peace Prize.

Twenty-two years after Williams and Corrigan received this recognition, the British and Irish governments finally came together with Northern Ireland political groups to sign the Good Friday Agreement. This treaty promised equality among all religious groups, and included a commitment to peaceful, democratic problem solving. "The Troubles" of Northern Ireland had finally come to an end.

Though war in their homeland has subsided, both Mairead Corrigan and Betty Williams remain active in peace work. These Irish activists continue to preach nonviolent responses to conflicts in other countries as well as their own.

"I believe that hope for the future depends on each of us taking nonviolence into our hearts and minds. . . . For those who say it cannot be done, let us remember that humanity learned to abolish slavery. Our task now is no less than the abolition of violence and war," Mairead Corrigan recently wrote. "We can rejoice and celebrate today because we are living in a miraculous time. Everything is changing and everything is possible."

NONVIOLENCE IS THE WEAPON OF THE STRONG. BETTY WILLIAMS

MAIREAD CORRIGAN. 1944–
BETTY WILLIAMS. 1943–

"The Troubles" was a long period of terrible violence between Protestant and Catholic paramilitary groups in Northern Ireland. Paramilitary groups are formed by ordinary people who take up arms without government approval. These groups often engage in terrorism, violence that is designed to scare and intimidate.

Trying to end paramilitary violence, Mairead Corrigan and Betty Williams organized a petition for peace. A petition is a statement signed by many people to show support for a cause. Most petitions are pieces of paper taken door-to-door, though many modern petitions can be found on the internet and are sent via e-mail.

Corrigan and Williams's work helped contribute to a peace treaty between the paramilitary groups. A treaty is an agreement between two warring groups or countries, promising not to fight. For their efforts Mairead Corrigan and Betty Williams were awarded the Nobel Peace Prize, the world's most prestigious international award for peace. Once a year the Nobel committee awards prizes of one million dollars to individuals who have contributed to the fields of physics, chemistry, physiology or medicine, literature, and peace.

Many other nonviolent activists have been nominated for or received Nobel Peace Prizes. Dr. Martin Luther King, Jr., won the Prize in 1964. In 1967 he nominated Thich Nhat Hanh in honor of his work against the Vietnam War. Nelson Mandela shared the prize with South African President F. W. de Klerk. Mohandas Gandhi was nominated five times but never won the award.

1977

BUENOS AIRES, ARGENTINA

THE BRICK PLAZA DE MAYO (*May Square*) *stretched out in front of the government palace of pink stone. It was a pleasant autumn day in April in the South American city. In the plaza middle-aged women with white triangular scarves tied over their hair strolled in pairs around the pyramid at the center of the plaza. They looked like ordinary women visiting with their friends.*

But as the women walked, police and soldiers watched. A constant threat was in the air. At any moment the women could be seized and beaten, jailed, tortured, or killed by the authorities. The women knew this all too well, because that's what had happened to their children. They gathered every Thursday afternoon from 3:30 to 4:00. They marched to draw attention to their disappeared children. Their desperation to find out what happened to their children overcame their fear.

IN MARCH OF 1976 Argentina had been taken over by a military coup, the violent overthrow of the government by a small group. The three officers who seized power formed a junta, a group that controlled the government, that promised to restore order to the troubled country. They would get rid of "subversion," they said. They would run the government by the values and morality of "Christianity, patriotism, and the family." This sounded like a good thing to most Argentine people. They had no idea what the junta actually had in mind: silencing anyone who seemed to be a threat. To the military leaders, "subversion" meant any action that suggested thinking differently from the way they did. Someone's "crime" could be working to improve conditions for poor people, demanding student rights, teaching, joining a labor union—or simply knowing someone who did any of these things.

Their method for silencing people was "disappearing" them. With no warning, unmarked cars pulled up to homes in the middle of the night. Brandishing guns, masked men grabbed sons or daughters, fathers or mothers, even young children, put hoods over their heads and drove them away. Most people were never seen again. This campaign came to be called the Dirty War. Over seven years as many as thirty thousand people disappeared in Argentina.

At first the mothers of disappeared people were very naive. Thinking there must have been some mistake, they went looking for their lost children. They knew they weren't subversives, but simply workers or students or teachers. The mothers were confident that their government would listen to them and return their children, or at least explain why they had been taken and where they were being held. The mothers went to police stations, detention centers, prisons, and government offices, searching and asking questions.

No matter where they went or whom they talked to, they never got any answers. As they searched they began to meet other mothers. They realized they weren't the only ones whose children had been taken. The mothers all shared a deep and terrible bond, the grief of losing their children.

WE NEEDED TO MEET IN A PUBLIC PLACE TO MAKE IT MORE DIFFICULT FOR THEM TO KIDNAP US. MARIA DEL ROSARIO

One of the group's members was Azucena Villaflor de Vincenti. Like the other mothers, she was a homemaker whose entire life revolved around taking care of her husband and children. Then her grown son Nestor was kidnapped.

De Vincenti and most of the other mothers had never done anything political before. Their losses and the frantic need to find out what had happened to their children gave them strength to take risks. They decided to force the military government to answer their questions by appearing in public. De Vincenti had the idea to go to the Plaza de Mayo because the Government House was there.

Fourteen mothers began gathering at the plaza, sitting on benches with their knitting and talking. Then they began to walk. "There were so few of us we were hardly noticed, and we had to make sure the public knew we existed. We wanted people to see us," one of the mothers later recalled. They decided to wear white scarves on their heads to identify themselves as a group.

The government wanted the mothers to remain invisible. The police threatened them, told them there was a law against any kind of group gathering. So they walked in pairs. On their white headscarves, they embroidered the names of their missing children.

When the mothers formed their group, each of the fourteen women was on a personal journey to find her own children. As their numbers grew, they became a movement on behalf of all disappeared people, the *desaparecidos*. They called themselves the Madres de Plaza de Mayo. The outside world came to know them as the Mothers of the Disappeared.

At first when the Mothers asked questions and protested, the military said their children were terrorists, threatening the country. The newspapers, controlled by the military, printed the same thing, and many Argentines accepted this explanation. Even churches closed their doors to the Mothers when they learned they were protesting against the government. Over months the Mothers were threatened and harassed by police and soldiers. Sometimes they were beaten as they gathered in the plaza. Many of them were arrested. Worst of all, several Mothers disappeared, including De Vincenti, the group's first leader.

During this time many Argentines, fearing for their lives, left the country to live in exile. They told stories of what was happening in Argentina. Reporters from other countries began asking questions. The military responded that the Mothers were just crazy old women, but the journalists kept asking questions. The story of the Mothers, walking around the Plaza de Mayo in their white scarves, began to be told around the world. In 1978 several Mothers traveled to the United States and to Italy, and later to other countries. They met with senators and congressmen, with presidents and religious leaders. They appeared at the United Nations and the Organization of American States. "We are the Mothers of the Disappeared from Buenos Aires, Argentina, and we are here to discuss human rights," they said to anyone who would listen.

In 1980 the group Madres de Plaza de Mayo was nominated for a Nobel Peace Prize. Although another human rights group in Argentina won the Nobel that year, the Mothers received a Peace Prize of the People from Norway.

By 1981 the military government was under serious pressure from other countries because of its human rights violations, which the Mothers had helped to publicize. Increasing troubles at home finally brought the government down. In 1983 a democratic government was elected. The Dirty War was over, but the work of the Mothers was not done. For twenty-two more years, they kept up their weekly walks, demanding that the people responsible for the disappearances be held accountable for their crimes. Much of the truth came out in a 1984 report from a commission of Argentinean citizens, which heard stories from thousands of people who had survived or witnessed the violence. Over the next two years a series of trials resulted in prison sentences for many of the highest-ranking military leaders found responsible, but many of the guilty escaped to other countries without punishment. The Mothers continued their marching in the plaza, demanding that the fugitives be brought to justice, but the group split over differing ideas of how to pursue their cause. Of the thousands of *desaparecidos,* the disappeared people, few were ever found, though some Mothers did discover what had happened to their children. Many were drugged and thrown out of helicopters into the sea, while others were buried in mass graves.

In 2006 the Mothers decided that they had aroused enough interest in their cause, and they were ready to turn to other important social issues.

The work of the Mothers and their incredible courage in facing an armed and repressive government inspired people all over the world. Today there are groups of Mothers and Families of the Disappeared in Chechnya and Russia; in Chile, Mexico, and El Salvador; in Kashmir and Nepal; and in other countries, demanding justice for their own missing children.

THE MOTHERS OF THE DISAPPEARED

Plaza de Mayo ("May Square" in Spanish) is a central square in Buenos Aires, Argentina—with a history of being used as a site for protests.

The Mothers's adult children who disappeared were accused of subversion—in this case, the act of speaking against or trying to undermine a political system from within. The junta responsible for the disappearances was made up of three military officers: an army general, a navy admiral, and an air force brigadier. Their control of the country was backed up by the force of all three branches of the military. They had the power to crush opposition from anyone. The disappearing of thirty thousand people by the junta was a terrible human rights violation in the eyes of the world. The Universal Declaration of Human Rights was passed by the United Nations in 1948. It states that "recognition of the inherent dignity and of the equal and inalienable rights of all members of the human family is the foundation of freedom, justice, and peace in the world." Global awareness of human rights violations in Argentina eventually helped to end the regime that ordered these horrific acts.

1989

A VILLAGE IN BURMA

THEY CAME WITHOUT WARNING, *six soldiers, all armed with rifles. Aung San Suu Kyi, the leader of the pro-democracy movement in Burma, was walking down a quiet village road when the troops appeared. A captain stood behind them, and at his orders the soldiers each crouched down and took aim at Suu Kyi and her small group of supporters.*

Reacting calmly, Aung San Suu Kyi waved her friends away.

She knew that the soldiers had come for her, and she didn't want anyone else to get hurt. Though sudden, the attack wasn't a total surprise; this was how the government dealt with troublemakers. Many other citizens who had stood up for democracy and human rights had been harassed, arrested, tortured, and killed by the brutal military regime, which had recently changed the official name of Suu Kyi's beloved country to "The Union of Myanmar."

Facing the soldiers, Suu Kyi could have done many things. She could have run away, or tried to beg for her life, or promised to stop fighting for democracy in Burma. Instead she simply continued walking down the road, ignoring the rifles that followed her.

Later she would write, "You should never let your fears prevent you from doing what you know is right."

Just before the soldiers would have shot her, an army officer stepped forward and stopped them. Perhaps he was afraid that Suu Kyi's death would only embolden the people of Burma, or perhaps he was moved by her bravery. In either case, Aung San Suu Kyi lived on to become Burma's greatest champion of democracy.

THE STRUGGLE ITSELF IS THE MOST IMPORTANT THING. I TELL OUR FOLLOWERS THAT WHEN WE ACHIEVE DEMOCRACY, WE WILL LOOK BACK WITH NOSTALGIA ON THE STRUGGLE AND HOW PURE WE WERE. AUNG SAN SUU KYI

AUNG SAN SUU KYI was the daughter of a Burmese hero, General Aung San. Her father was famous for negotiating with the British to gain independence for the country of Burma. Suu Kyi's young life was full of sad losses. Her father was assassinated when she was two years old, only months before he was supposed to become the leader of an independent Burmese nation. Eight years later, her brother drowned in a pond.

After gaining independence from the United Kingdom in 1948, Burma was known as "The Union of Burma." In 1962, when Suu Kyi was seventeen, General Ne Win violently overthrew the democratically elected president of Burma and replaced him with a brutal junta, a military dictatorship. Anyone who resisted the new government was arrested, expelled from the country, or killed. The military would take people from their homes to do unpaid, hard labor building bridges or railroads. Because of her family's stature, Suu Kyi was spared this oppression. As the ambassador to India, Aung San Suu Kyi's mother was able to take her children out of the country to live in New Delhi after the junta took power.

The teenage Aung San Suu Kyi was an avid learner. In addition to studying political science and learning cooking, piano, horseback riding, and Japanese, Suu Kyi studied the nonviolent teachings of Gandhi.

She put these tactics to work twenty-six years later,

when she finally returned to Burma to care for her dying mother in 1988. In the intervening years she had married, had children, studied at Oxford, and worked for the United Nations. Aung San Suu Kyi didn't plan on becoming a freedom fighter, but destiny had other plans for her.

Aung San Suu Kyi returned to a Burma that was in chaos. People were demonstrating for freedom, but the regime was responding by arresting, torturing, and killing protesters. There was no freedom of the press, no freedom of public gathering. When word got out that General Aung San's daughter had returned, people took it as a sign that Burma would once again be free.

A few months after she returned home, Aung San Suu Kyi stood on the Shwedagon Pagoda and addressed a crowd of five hundred thousand demonstrators. It was the same spot where her father had stood just over forty years earlier, speaking about Burmese independence. Suu Kyi declared the importance of three values: nonviolence, human rights, and democracy.

She continued speaking out and chose to stay in Burma instead of returning to her family and career. She refused to be deterred by the threats of the government, until finally they put her under house arrest. The government offered to release her, if she would leave the country. In response she said, "You will have to drag me to the airport in chains."

In 1990 the military regime held a supposedly free election, but the election was a fraud. Aung San Suu Kyi's party, the National League for Democracy, won an astonishing 82 percent of the seats, but the existing government simply refused to give up its power.

The next year Aung San Suu Kyi was awarded the Nobel Peace Prize. She used the prize money to improve health and education in Burma.

Today Aung San Suu Kyi remains under house arrest. Her husband died in 1999, and her children remain in the United Kingdom. She hasn't seen them in eighteen years, because they aren't allowed into Burma, and if their mother leaves the country to see them, she can never return. Though Burma is ruled by new leaders, the military dictatorship remains in power, and they harshly attack anyone who even mentions Aung San Suu Kyi. Instead, the people refer to her as "the Lady."

YOU SHOULD NEVER LET YOUR FEARS PREVENT YOU FROM DOING WHAT YOU KNOW IS RIGHT. AUNG SAN SUU KYI

AUNG SAN SUU KYI. 1945-

Aung San Suu Kyi has spent much of her life under house arrest. House arrest is a way for governments to punish or control people without putting them in jail or killing them. By locking Suu Kyi in her house, the Myanmar government is able to keep her out of sight without exposing her to the hardships of jail. Since she is a much-loved national icon, the government is afraid of the Burmese people's response if her health were to deteriorate from the harsh conditions of imprisonment.

The choice Aung San Suu Kyi faced when the government offered to release her must have been excruciating. By refusing, she was giving up the chance to be with her family, but she knew that if she left the country, never allowed to return, she would be abandoning her people and the cause of democracy. Still under house arrest in Burma, Aung San Suu Kyi stands as a symbol of nonviolent resistance to the people of Burma and the world.

In the fall of 2007, thousands of Buddhist monks, joined by other citizens, took to the streets of Yangon to oppose the military junta and show support for Aung San Suu Kyi. Though this protest ended in violent repression, with activists being killed or jailed, it showed the world that the people of Burma continue to oppose their government.

1989

BEIJING, CHINA

"THE ARMY IS COMING!" *The shout echoed up and down Tiananmen Square. Though it was the largest plaza on Earth, the square could barely contain the hundreds of thousands of Chinese students who had come to protest for democracy. For over a month the students had refused the government's orders to disperse. They had raised banners and tents and even erected a giant statute they called the Goddess of Democracy. Twice before the army had come to remove them, and twice the soldiers had been pushed back by a living wall of students and workers. Now the military was back, a massive, rumbling convoy of tanks and trucks filled with armed soldiers.*

The students remained firm. They had sworn an oath the night before: "Our blood can be shed, but we will not lose the People's Square. We will fight to the end with the last person." As the soldiers approached, people filled the streets, preventing the Army from going forward. As they had done before, the protesters shouted at the soldiers:

"Why would you come to attack us? We are fighting for your rights, too!"

At first the convoys slowed and waited in front of the masses. Then, without warning, trucks and tanks sped forward, smashing through barriers and running people over. Soldiers dismounted and began firing, first over the protesters' heads, and then at them. Tear gas bombs sent burning smoke clouds drifting through the streets.

Many of the crowd panicked and ran, while others stood fast. At one point a single young man stood in front of an advancing column of tanks, holding his ground even though others had been run over. The lead tank tried to drive around him, but he moved to block them. This strange dance continued until finally the man crawled up on top of the vehicle and started shouting at the soldiers.

Eventually the soldiers arrived at Tiananmen Square, leaving a trail of death and devastation behind them. As trucks and tanks converged on the students, the government shut off power to the square. Soon the only light came from burning vehicles in the distance. As the square was slowly but steadily cleared, a tank drove into and over the Goddess of Democracy, crushing it. The government had retaken the People's Square, but only by waging a war against its own citizens.

IT HAD ALL STARTED with a few thousand students, marching to demand freedom of the press, an end to government repression, and free elections. At the time, China was run by an oppressive, corrupt regime that was intolerant of criticism. Anyone who spoke out was arrested or attacked. But the people had had enough.

Soon the small crowd of students became a mass of protesters. As the pro-democracy movement swept the country, the students were joined by middle-aged workers, mothers carrying babies, and the elderly. All across China people were engaging in strikes and protests in support of the Tiananmen Square demonstration. The government became worried. They sent the police, then the military, to remove the protesters by force. Each time the people refused to give up the square, and the government forces were ordered to stand down.

The protesters believed that nonviolence was key to their success. One student leader would later recall that when some people began arming themselves with rocks, pipes, and sharpened bamboo sticks, "The students from headquarters told everybody that we represented a peaceful movement and its highest principle was sacrifice. We knew that this was a war between love and hatred, not between force and force."

Though the Chinese students were silenced, their message was heard around the world. Thanks to foreign journalists, the photograph of one young man stopping a tank column became an icon of nonviolent dissent. Tiananmen Square was the largest student movement in the history of the world, with over six million participating from over six hundred colleges and universities. The Chinese government's response crushed the hopes of the students and all those who longed for democracy, but the students' extraordinary bravery and passionate defiance has inspired activists across the globe to take a stand against government repression. Someday the students' actions may be remembered as the beginning of a movement that united China in a participatory form of government.

STUDENT ACTIVISTS OF TIANANMEN SQUARE

The student activists at Tiananmen Square were fighting for participatory democracy, which is a government where the people have a voice. At the time, Chinese citizens had no choice in the election of their leaders and were not allowed to criticize the oppressive, corrupt Communist Party. Anyone who dared to speak out against the government was intimidated, arrested, or attacked.

To repress the gatherings of activists in 1989, the Chinese government had to send the military out all over the country. When military forces are on the move, they travel in convoys, or formations of vehicles. One tool that government forces all over the world have used to repress protests is tear gas. It is a non-lethal weapon that makes the eyes and skin burn, forcing crowds to break up.

Tiananmen Square was not the only place where Chinese students and workers gathered to protest in the spring of 1989. There were also protests in most major Chinese cities, including Chongqing, Changsa, and Shanghai.

WE KNEW THIS WAS A WAR BETWEEN LOVE AND HATRED, NOT BETWEEN FORCE AND FORCE. A PRO-DEMOCRACY STUDENT LEADER

1989. BEIJING, CHINA

CAPE TOWN, SOUTH AFRICA

HUNDREDS OF PEOPLE *filled the pews of St. George's Cathedral, where they had fled to escape police. Black, white, Indian, "Colored," church people, unionists, teachers, journalists, and many others had joined together in a peaceful protest. As the people marched, police blocked their way, hitting them with whips and batons and turning on a water cannon that knocked marchers over and blasted them with purple dye. They arrested hundreds, carting them away by the truckload. Now the police waited outside, surrounding the church. Archbishop Desmond Tutu, the highest-ranking black Anglican priest in South Africa, addressed the people. As usual Tutu included the white police in his vision of the future.*

"The prize for which we are striving is freedom, is freedom for all of us, freedom for those people standing

outside, freedom for them! Because, you see, when we are free, when we are free, they will be here, they will be here, joining with us celebrating that freedom, and not standing outside there stopping us from becoming free."

He addressed the white leaders of the nation, asking them to "come here and look at what South Africa will become, what South Africa is going to become. Just look at all these beautiful people. Do you really think that these are terrorists? Do you really think that these are violent people? Why do you use violence?"

His voice rising and falling, his speech punctuated with humor, his eyes sparkling, Archbishop Tutu exhorted his people not to be downcast. "Now straighten up your shoulders, come, straighten up your shoulders like people who were born for freedom! Lovely, lovely, lovely!"

DESMOND TUTU didn't begin his priesthood with an intention of getting involved in politics. Tutu's father, mother, and grandmother came from three different tribes. Tutu spoke three languages as a young boy, and saw himself as an African—a South African—rather than a member of a particular tribe. When he was eight his father took a new teaching job and moved the family to a town where Tutu soon learned his fourth language, Afrikaans, the language of the ruling white majority. Now he could understand the name-calling and rude comments that whites sometimes directed at him.

He was disturbed to see his father being stopped by police demanding to see the pass that all black South Africans had to carry. The aim of the apartheid system was to secure the best land and resources for white citizens and to completely separate blacks from areas where whites lived. The pass system allowed the white minority to rigidly control the movement of black citizens, even though they outnumbered whites four to one.

Although his father had a respected position as a teacher, the Tutus, like most black South Africans, earned very low wages and were forced to live in houses that had no electricity, no sewage system, and often no running water. White schools had government lunch programs, but black schools didn't, so his family scraped money together for him to buy snacks. Tutu went about barefoot,

I BELIEVE HISTORY TEACHES US A CATEGORICAL LESSON: THAT ONCE A PEOPLE ARE DETERMINED TO BECOME FREE, THEN NOTHING IN THE WORLD CAN STOP THEM REACHING THEIR GOAL. DESMOND TUTU

inventing schemes with his friends to earn a little money. Despite his poverty Tutu was a brilliant student who was always at the top of his class.

When he was fourteen Tutu caught tuberculosis, a disease of the lungs. He spent nearly two years in the hospital, and there he made a friend who changed his life. Father Trevor Huddleston was a white priest who came to visit the young black boy every week, bringing him books to read. Father Huddleston loved his conversations with this bright and engaging boy. The priest's attention and Tutu's long illness caused him to deepen his belief as a Christian and to begin a lifetime of talking and listening to God.

WE MUST NOT ONLY SPEAK ABOUT FORGIVENESS AND RECONCILIATION— WE MUST ACT ON THESE PRINCIPLES. DESMOND TUTU

Tutu wanted to study to be a doctor but couldn't afford the fees, so he chose to become a teacher instead. This career was cut short when the government created Bantu education, a separate system for blacks with the goal of training them only as servants and laborers. Unable to support such a system, Tutu quit teaching.

He decided to become a priest in the Anglican Church. At first he concentrated on becoming a pastor who cared for his people, and on furthering his education. Traveling to England to study in 1962, he and his family were amazed by the experience of being treated as ordinary human beings. They could walk about freely with no passes, could go through any public entrance, could attend any school. His time in England convinced Tutu that the fight in South Africa needed to be against the system of apartheid, not against white people.

Over the years Tutu kept receiving appointments to higher and higher positions. With each one he had a bigger stage from which to speak out to the nation of South Africa, and to people in other countries.

While Nelson Mandela was fighting injustice from within the prison system, Desmond Tutu was challenging it on the outside with fierce and enthusiastic eloquence. Completely committed to nonviolence and preaching a message of reconciliation between races, Tutu became the world's best-known spokesperson against apartheid.

In 1984 he was awarded the Nobel Peace Prize. The award put him in a spotlight in front of the entire world. He called for countries and companies to take their money and business away from South Africa until apartheid was ended. These sanctions were one factor that pressured the government to abandon the system of apartheid.

Perhaps the most challenging job Tutu ever took on came after black Africans had gained the vote and elected Nelson Mandela as president. A new South Africa had been formed, but if the nation was to move forward, the wounds of apartheid needed to be healed. Instead of trying to punish people for their crimes, the new leaders envisioned an entirely new form of justice. Those who had been harmed under apartheid were invited to tell their stories to the Truth and Reconciliation Commission. Anyone who confessed wrongdoing would be given amnesty instead of a prison sentence. Archbishop Tutu became the chairperson of the Commission. The four years of its work were painfully difficult, but the Commission gave the world a new vision of peaceful progress.

DESMOND TUTU. 1931–

South Africa's program of "Bantu Education" was a product of the distorted thinking of apartheid. The term "Bantu" is the name of an African language group, but white South Africans used it as a negative way to describe black people of all tribes or clans. Those who designed the Bantu Education system believed that black Africans were inferior by nature, suited only for service jobs and physical work. They claimed that it wasn't fair to educate blacks for positions in life that they wouldn't be able to hold. Instead they created a program that would only teach skills and information for jobs serving whites. It was a way of making sure that black South Africans couldn't qualify for higher positions.

Even amidst the evils of apartheid, Desmond Tutu always tried to bring people together. He practiced reconciliation, a process of getting past differences and injustices in order to restore relationships. This is why he was chosen to head the Truth and Reconciliation Commission, which was designed to reveal past crimes and allow victims to heal without creating more violence. Many people also finally learned what had happened to family members and friends who had disappeared.

South Africa's Truth and Reconciliation Commission was based on truth commissions formed in a number of Latin American countries, including Argentina's 1984 citizen commission. The process developed in South Africa made some significant changes, received international attention, and became a model for healing from conflict and violence that has been used all over the world by countries such as Liberia, Sierra Leone, Morocco, South Korea, Nepal, Indonesia, Peru, and Canada, and by the city of Greensboro, North Carolina.

1989

PRAGUE, CZECHOSLOVAKIA

IN A CRAMPED DRESSING ROOM *of the Magic Lantern theater, a group of men huddled together, talking. Karate students guarded the labyrinth of hallways, only admitting the ballet dancers who came to serve coffee and sandwiches. The Civic Forum, as they called themselves, was a strange group, made up of artists, intellectuals, rock stars, religious leaders, and political organizers. Though they met in a theater and were led by a playwright, they did not gather to discuss drama.*

They were plotting a revolution.

The Civic Forum met in secret because the repressive government tried to crush anyone who spoke out against them. The government had soldiers, secret police, guns, and tanks. Similar meetings had been raided, and other dissidents had been harassed, beaten, and taken away by the secret police. From time to time there would be a rumor that someone had planted a bomb in the basement, but the Civic Forum would work on anyway. They couldn't afford to be afraid of attacks. Though the odds seemed hopeless, they lived by the words of their leader, Václav Havel: "Politics is the art of the impossible."

I REALLY DO INHABIT A SYSTEM IN WHICH WORDS ARE CAPABLE OF SHAKING THE ENTIRE STRUCTURE OF GOVERNMENT, WHERE WORDS CAN PROVE MIGHTIER THAN TEN MILITARY DIVISIONS. VÁCLAV HAVEL

HAVEL WAS A FAMOUS playwright and hero of the intellectual underground. He had been just a boy when the communist Soviet Union took control of Czechoslovakia. Havel came from an upper-class family of architects, but when the new government seized power, everything was taken away. The communists believed that wealth should be evenly distributed, though in practice it often ended up in the hands of the new leaders. Even though his family had lost their wealth, Havel was discriminated against because of his privileged background, and he wasn't allowed to continue school past age fifteen. Havel went to work at a lab instead and started taking night courses. After a two-year stint in the military, Havel began to pursue his real love, theater. For years he worked as a stagehand, lighting technician, producer, and secretary. He was also writing, and his first three plays earned him worldwide acclaim.

In 1968 everything changed. The president of Czechoslovakia, Alexander Dubcek, decided that the country should have independence from the Soviet Union. In response, the Soviet Union invaded.

Havel was with his wife, Olga, in the town of Liberec when the Soviet Army arrived in August of 1968. Tanks smashed through buildings, and some soldiers fired randomly into crowds of fleeing people. Disguised as a factory worker in a cap and overalls, Havel stayed in the town to write radio broadcasts condemning the occupation and encouraging the Czech people to resist nonviolently. Eventually, though, Dubcek was replaced with a new, harsher Soviet puppet government.

One of the new government's first acts in power was to crack down on the intellectual community. Anything new or untraditional was considered dangerous. Books, music, essays, journals, and plays were quickly banned, including Havel's works.

These new laws provoked an underground of artists and intellectuals who had been persecuted by the government. These rebels of the mind taught classes in basements, held concerts in the woods, and found ways to publish their own writings. In 1975 Havel showed one of his banned plays, *The Beggar's Opera,* in the back room of a pub for one night.

It was the Plastic People of the Universe, however, that these dissidents rallied around. The Plastics were a band of musicians that the government saw as too subversive. Their unusual, experimental musical style embodied everything that the Czech regime was afraid of. At first the government simply revoked the band's license to perform, and had police beat and harass their supporters. But in 1976, when the Plastic People of the Universe continued to play, the government had them arrested.

The artistic community was outraged that anyone could

be jailed simply for playing music. People joined together to organize a defense, and out of that campaign came Charter 77, an illegally distributed petition demanding human rights in Czechoslovakia. Havel and others were arrested in a dramatic police raid in 1977 while distributing the petitions. This was Havel's first jail sentence of many to come. Over the next decade Havel was arrested countless times and spent over four years in prison. His family was harassed and persecuted; he was publicly shamed. Still he fought on. Then, in 1989, his twenty years of work and sacrifice paid off, when the Czech people rose in revolution.

After so many years of struggle, the revolution happened with astonishing speed. Despite rumors that troops were moving into the city, two hundred thousand demonstrators came to hear Havel speak on November 21, 1989. Daily demonstrations were taking place in Prague, with numbers rapidly swelling. On the 25th, seven hundred fifty thousand people gathered and were treated to the news that key members of the government were resigning. The next day nearly one million Czech people gathered in the freezing plaza. Addressing them, Havel said: "We want truth, humanity, freedom. . . . From here on we are all directing this country of ours and all of us bear responsibility for its fate."

Two weeks later the prime minister resigned. Because

the transition of power came with no violence, the movement organized by Havel and the other Czech intellectuals came to be known as the Velvet Revolution. Not long
after that Havel was resoundingly elected the new president of Czechoslovakia. The small circle of dissidents had
indeed proven themselves artists of the impossible.

In January of 1990, only a few months after the Civic
Forum had begun to meet in a smoky dressing room,
Vaclav Havel made his first speech as president of Czechoslovakia. Speaking frankly, he told the now-free citizens
that there was much work to be done. He concluded his
speech by saying: "People, your government has returned
to you."

POLITICS CAN BE NOT ONLY THE ART OF THE POSSIBLE . . . IT CAN BE THE ART OF THE IMPOSSIBLE. VACLAV HAVEL

VÁCLAV HAVEL. 1936–

During the Velvet Revolution Václav Havel was part of the Czech intellectual underground. An intellectual is someone who is given to study, reflection, and speculation. A political movement is called "underground" when it has to stay hidden from the government in power with which it disagrees. Members of an underground movement are often called dissidents. In the case of Havel and the other Czech dissidents, they had to keep their activities secret because of government persecution. The government attempted to intimidate or harm citizens for their political beliefs. The government also kept lists of individuals they labeled as dissident or dangerous, and these people were often arrested or fired from their jobs. When a person gets this type of negative attention from the government, they have been "blacklisted."

Havel and the other dissidents of the Velvet Revolution created Charter 77, a petition demanding democracy and criticizing the Czech Communist Party as a puppet government. A puppet government is one that is set up and directed by a foreign government. In the case of Czechoslovakia, which claimed to be independent, the government was actually controlled by the Soviet Union.

Four years after Havel became president, Czechoslovakia split into the Czech Republic and Slovakia. Havel remained president of the Czech Republic another ten years, until 2003.

NAIROBI, KENYA

TENTS HAD BEEN SET UP *on the edge of Uhuru Park (Freedom Park), a green space in the middle of the busy city. A group of older women, wrapped in traditional patterned cloths, had gathered there. They called it "Freedom Corner." Most were from the countryside. They didn't know how to read or write, but they knew that the government had arrested their sons. Some had been held in jail for more than two years. Their only crime was opposing the government's misuse of power. The mothers had begun a hunger strike on behalf of the political prisoners. They planned to stay in the park, fasting, until their family members were released.*

Day after day, more people arrived, joining the encampment or standing on the sides with signs supporting the mothers' action. President Daniel arap Moi, who had ruled Kenya as a dictator for fourteen years, was not pleased to have the women in the park, attracting attention, protesting, and criticizing his government.

On the fourth day police arrived on horseback with

dogs and tear gas. They charged into the crowd, clubbing people with nightsticks and threatening them with guns. Newspapers around the world reported that four members of the group were knocked unconscious, including a woman named Wangari Maathai.

WE ARE CALLED TO ASSIST THE EARTH TO HEAL HER WOUNDS AND IN THE PROCESS HEAL OUR OWN—INDEED, TO EMBRACE THE WHOLE CREATION IN ALL ITS DIVERSITY, BEAUTY, AND WONDER. WANGARI MAATHAI

WANGARI MAATHAI, known as the "Tree Lady," was born in Nyeri, Kenya. Her family was part of the Kikuyu tribe, what Maathai likes to call a "micro-nation." They lived in the highlands among rolling hills. When she was a girl, Maathai often walked to the nearby stream to fill water pails for her family. She took long drinks of the pure, clear water. She poked at frogs' eggs and watched tadpoles swimming. All around her, the land was green, shaded by tall trees. Her family owned little, but they always had plenty to eat from the crops they grew themselves.

As she grew, Maathai attended school, an unusual experience for a young girl in the Kenyan highlands in the 1940s. She won a scholarship to study biology at an American college and spent the early 1960s in the United States, during the time of the American civil rights movement.

Returning to Kenya, she earned her Ph.D. in veterinary medicine from the University of Nairobi. She was the first woman in East and Central Africa to earn such an advanced degree. Maathai began teaching veterinary anatomy and rose to become the first African woman to head a university department.

In 1975 the United Nations planned the first-ever conference to hear the concerns of the world's women. They asked every member nation to listen to women and report the information gathered to the conference in Mexico

City. To gather information for her report, Wangari Maathai went into the countryside to hear the stories of the women of Kenya. They told of their hard lives, their need for firewood, the lack of clean drinking water, the scarcity of good food to eat.

Trained as a scientist, Maathai looked for the causes of the problems. She saw that the forests of Kenya had been cut down in many places, and that the lack of trees was often the main reason that people couldn't meet their basic needs. Without tree roots, soil washed away in heavy rains and ran into the streams and rivers, muddying them. Without tree shade the remaining soil dried out in the sun and couldn't hold water. Streams dried up. The plants that people and animals depended on for food died. As the land turned to desert, people had to walk farther and farther to find clean water and firewood.

The solution Maathai came up with was to plant trees. She set up a program to train women to raise, plant, and care for seedlings. For each one that survived, the women would be paid. This would give them much-needed income with which they could send their children to school. On June 5, 1977, World Environmental Day, Maathai and a group of women planted seven trees. The Green Belt Movement was born.

To Maathai the tree symbolized peace, the peace that is possible when people care for the land in such a way that it can sustain them. She remembered the Kikuyu elders carrying wooden staffs made of the thigi tree. When an elder placed the staff between people who were having an argument, they would stop fighting and find a way to solve their conflict. She also believed that as women were successful at planting trees, they would solve the other problems in their lives, too.

In 1978 President Moi came into power. His political party took complete control of Kenya. They were disturbed to see women organizing and taking things into their own hands. They feared that the Green Belt Movement would threaten their hold on the country. They made it illegal to meet in groups of more than nine.

"The tree became a symbol for the democratic struggle in Kenya," Maathai said. The government tried to stop the women from planting trees by criticizing, arresting, and beating them. Some people who spoke out, men and women, were tortured or even killed.

Maathai survived her 1992 beating and many arrests. Though the Mothers' Hunger Strike finally forced the release of political prisoners, it took another ten years of work and protests before the government of President Moi was defeated. In 2002 a new president was elected in a democratic process. Maathai won a seat in parliament and the new president appointed her to the post of assistant environmental minister.

In 2004 Wangari Maathai received the Nobel Peace Prize. She was the first African woman and the first environmentalist to win the award. Maathai sees a direct connection between management of the environment and peace. "If we were to accept as a human family to manage our resources more sustainably, more responsibly, more accountably, if we were to agree to share them more equitably," she has said, "we would be able to reduce conflict."

Since 1977 the women of the Green Belt Movement have planted more than forty million trees in Kenya. The movement has spread to other countries in Africa and other continents. In 2007, in a global collaboration with the Green Belt Movement, one billion trees were planted around the world.

WANGARI MAATHAI. 1940-

Like Gandhi and many who came after him, Wangari Maathai spent time as a political prisoner. Political prisoners are jailed because they have stood against those in power. Their "crimes" might be joining an organization, attending a meeting, or writing a piece critical of the government.

President Daniel arap Moi imposed a dictatorship that attempted to silence anyone who opposed him. Only one political party was allowed. The president's party, or group, decided how the country would be run. They chose the members of parliament, the representatives who made laws. They didn't allow other political parties to meet or to offer leaders for people to vote for in elections. President Moi and his party were right to fear those speaking out against their control of the country, because as soon as other political parties were allowed and an election was held, his party was defeated.

Although Wangari Maathai was the first environmentalist to receive the Nobel Peace Prize, there is growing recognition of the connection between the environment, justice, and peace. In 2007 former US Vice President Al Gore and the Intergovernmental Panel on Climate Change, a group of scientists, won the Nobel Peace Prize for their work to increase knowledge and promote action to prevent global warming.

ROME. TOKYO. MOSCOW. JOHANNESBURG. MEXICO CITY. ISTANBUL. PARIS. TEL AVIV. NEW YORK CITY. BERLIN. BAGHDAD. BUDAPEST. HONG KONG. AND HUNDREDS OF OTHER CITIES . . .

. . . ACROSS THE PLANET

ON FEBRUARY 15, 2003, *the world said no to war. Using the Internet, hundreds of organizations were able to coordinate millions of people for one massive global protest. It was the largest nonviolent demonstration the world had ever seen. No one knows exactly how many people were involved, but estimates range from six to thirty million. The protesters were students, grandmothers, artists, businessmen and women, celebrities, nuns, veterans, children. In many languages, they spoke with one voice: "No War On Iraq!"*

Some protests were tiny. On an isolated international station in Antarctica, a few dozen scientists held a rally on the ice. Other protests were huge. In London over a million people gathered in the largest demonstration ever held in the United Kingdom. They carried signs with such sayings as, "Don't Attack Iraq" and "Make Tea Not War."

In New York City Archbishop Desmond Tutu addressed hundreds of thousands of protesters. "How can we say we want to drop bombs on our sisters and broth-

ers, on our children?" he asked. "President Bush, listen to the voice of the people, for many times the voice of the people is the voice of God," Tutu said. "Listen to the voice of the people saying, 'Give peace a chance.'"

President George W. Bush and the US government didn't listen. On March 20th, 2003, American troops invaded Iraq. The war devastated the country and claimed hundreds of thousands of lives, most of them innocent. Tens of thousands of American soldiers have been wounded or killed.

IT IS THE ACID TEST OF NONVIOLENCE THAT... THERE IS NO RANCOR LEFT BEHIND, AND IN THE END, THE ENEMIES ARE CONVERTED INTO FRIENDS. MOHANDAS GANDHI

THE FUTURE OF NONVIOLENCE

THE WORLD NEEDS PEOPLE like Gandhi. Astonishing changes have happened in the last one hundred years, but there is still much injustice and violence in the world. On every continent governments or groups are trying to displace or destroy people simply because of their skin color, religion, or ethnic group. Countries continue to persecute their own citizens. People are still imprisoned not for actual crimes, but for their beliefs or ideas. Many countries are ravaged by war. Pollution, poverty, and terrible working conditions cause suffering all over the world.

Fortunately, new tools for nonviolent activists are being discovered all the time. Advances in communication technology have created the possibility for worldwide movements. Thanks to cell phones and email, Ukrainian activists were able to gather hundreds of thousands of people to protest rigged elections in Kiev. This "smart mobbing" was also used in the Philippines, where masses of Filipino people assembled to force the corrupt president to step down in 2001.

Another important development is the popularization of online blogs, which allow activists to share news that might not be covered by big media. Websites and chatrooms promote the sharing of ideas and strategies across continents, creating global networks of activists.

One example of this international solidarity was the "Intergalactica" conference held in the jungles of Chiapas, Mexico. During this historic meeting thousands of activists came from all over the world to meet and discuss strategies of resistance against global corporations and increasing inequality. The conference was organized by the Zapatistas, a movement of indigenous Mayans fighting for self-determination and economic equality.

As they did in organizing protests against the invasion of Iraq, people across the globe can now work together to solve a problem that affects the whole world. Environmental activists working in different countries use computer networks to share information about their efforts to save the earth from global warming, nuclear arms, and the extinction of plants and animals. The struggle for human rights unites activists around the world working for gay rights, against torture, and on behalf of political prisoners. Other global movements oppose the power of corporations and demand better working conditions and wages for workers in every country. When large international companies meet, these "anti-globalization" activists come from all over the world to protest.

Like Gandhi, we can only imagine what other forms nonviolent resistance may take. By learning about the work of Gandhi and those who came after him, you are already part of the future of nonviolent resistance. What are your ideas? How might you get involved?

WE ARE CONSTANTLY BEING ASTONISHED THESE DAYS AT THE AMAZING DISCOVERIES IN THE FIELD OF VIOLENCE. BUT I MAINTAIN THAT FAR MORE UNDREAMT OF AND SEEMINGLY IMPOSSIBLE DISCOVERIES WILL BE MADE IN THE FIELD OF NONVIOLENCE. MOHANDAS GANDHI

AUTHORS' NOTE

THE BUILDING is a cement-floored warehouse on the outskirts of Mobile, Alabama. On this sultry March night in 2006, a crowd of nearly one hundred has gathered to prepare for a journey—The Veterans and Survivors March for Peace and Justice: "Walkin' to New Orleans." Listening to instructions and loading up supplies, we are a group of contrasts. Middle-aged veterans of the Vietnam War in camouflage green, some with white hair and beards, work beside trim young soldiers in khaki desert camouflage. Relatives and supporters, mostly white, who have flown in from our comfortable homes in California, Colorado, and Maine, mingle with African American residents of the Gulf Coast who survived Hurricane Katrina.

We have a common purpose that brings us together across our differences of age, class, and race. Starting tomorrow, on foot and in bus caravan, we will travel the length of the Gulf Coast from Mobile to New Orleans. Our purpose is to broadcast a message: Stop the war and bring people home. We mean to connect the war in Iraq with the devastation of the Gulf Coast following Hurricane Katrina. Six months after the disaster, so many people are still homeless, so many places still destroyed. What if our government were to take the money we are spending on the war in another country and spend it on reconstructing our own country? Bring the soldiers home from Iraq and send them instead to rebuild the Gulf Coast. Bring the displaced people home to Mississippi, Alabama, and Louisiana.

We joined the march as a mother-son team, Perry as a veteran of Afghanistan and a member of Iraq Veterans Against the War (IVAW) and Anne as a family supporter and a member of Military Families Speak Out. Carrying signs and banners and chanting cadences, we walked along city streets, down country highways, and over broken pavement along a devastated stretch of coast. Along the way we stopped for rest breaks and press conferences. At night we camped in tent cities pitched in the yards of African American and Vietnamese churches, and once at a work camp on the banks of a Louisiana bayou. We lined up for communal meals cooked over oil drum fires and for bucket showers in blue tarp stalls. We used a set of port-a-potties towed by a caravan truck. Along the way our numbers grew. A man left homeless and jobless by the hurricane joined our community. Residents welcomed us as we came to their towns, then marched alongside us the rest of the journey.

Most significantly, we listened to peoples' stories. Katrina survivors spoke of harrowing survival in the storm, of losing homes and finding neighbors dead, and the suffering that continued six months later as people still waited for relief. Young veterans told of the cost of war on their own lives: the violence of battle, seeing enemy soldiers, Iraqi children, or their own buddies wounded or killed, and suffering mental anguish and anxiety attacks months and years after their service ended. Parents, including activist Cindy Sheehan, shared their devastating grief at the loss of their children, killed in the war.

Six days later, dirty, tired, footsore, and with full hearts, we walked into New Orleans three hundred strong on the third anniversary of the invasion of Iraq.

As we write this note, long after the march, funding continues to flow to the war in Iraq, and the Gulf Coast continues to struggle to rebuild. Another thousand US soldiers and tens of thousands of Iraqi citizens have died. There is no sign that our weeklong action had any impact whatsoever on the policies of our government.

Like our march, most nonviolent resistance is a matter of simply taking the next step, putting one foot in front of each other, on a long journey. Clear signs of significant changes are rare, but there are other signs we can observe.

As we researched the last hundred years of nonviolence, we began to notice a series of recurring themes, commonalities that showed up in story after story. This is the wisdom we can gain from these pioneers of nonviolent strategies. We can benefit from what they discovered and use what they have to teach us so that we can continue the struggle for a peaceful and just world.

On our march Perry used his background as an army medic to serve on the medical team, bandaging blisters, handing out sunscreen, and making sure that people drank enough water. Anne carried extra rations of dried fruit, nuts, and granola bars to share with anyone who needed an energy boost. The lessons we take from the pioneers of nonviolent resistance can be like the bandages or snacks we carry along for the journey. From their lives we can draw hope and courage to keep going, even when there is no evidence that we are accomplishing anything. And as people continue to seek nonviolent resolutions to war and injustice, one day someone will read in this book about the Iraq War and other conflicts to which we can't yet imagine a solution, and it will be a piece of history, a conflict of the past.

BIBLIOGRAPHY

Gene Sharp's comprehensive categorization of *The Methods of Nonviolence* (Manchester, NH: Porter Sargent, 1998) gave us an important overview of the field as we began our research. We referred frequently to Peter Ackerman and Jack DuVall's *A Force More Powerful: A Century of Nonviolent Conflict* (New York: Palgrave Macmillan, 2001), a compelling narrative account of many of the most significant nonviolent movements of the twentieth century.

Whenever possible we started the exploration of each individual with an autobiography, learning about the person's life as they experienced it, in their own words. Gandhi's autobiography, *The Story of My Experiments with Truth,* translated from the Gujarati by Mahadev Desai (Ahmedabad, India: Navajivan Publishing House, 1929), however, has only a few details of the early actions he led in South Africa. We found these details, especially descriptions of the August 16, 1908, mass burning of registration certificates, in a group of titles from the Olin Library at Cornell University: *Gandhi in South Africa: British Imperialism and the Indian Question, 1860–1914* (Ithaca: Cornell University Press, 1971) by Robert Huttenback; *Gandhi and South Africa* by Shanti Sadiq Ali (Delhi: Hind Pocket Books, 1994); and *Gandhi: The South African Experience* by Maureen Swan (Johannesburg: Ravan Press, 1985). We were thrilled to discover in Swan's book an actual photograph of the August 16, 1908, event we describe. We also found helpful details in the first biography of Gandhi, *M. K. Gandhi: An Indian Patriot in South Africa* (Delhi Publications Division, Ministry of Information and Broadcasting, Government of India, 1967. First published 1909). Written by Joseph J. Doke, a British journalist, the book is based on extensive interviews with Gandhi in South Africa. These interviews filled in the particulars of Gandhi's childhood and his earliest religious and philosophical influences. Dennis Dalton's *Mahatma Gandhi: Nonviolent Power in Action* (New York: Columbia University Press, 1993) was useful for its in-depth discussion of the origins and meaning of *satyagraha*.

Thich Nhat Hanh's book, *Fragrant Palm Leaves: Journals, 1962–1966* (New York: Riverhead Trade, 1999) offered journal entries from the Vietnam War era. *Thich Nhat Hanh: Essential Writings*, edited by Robert Ellsberg

(Maryknoll, NY: Orbis Books, 2001), gave important insight into Thich Nhat Hanh's particular brand of engaged, socially active Buddhism.

An essay, "The Real Rosa Parks," by Paul Rogat Loeb, in the collection he edited, *The Impossible Will Take a Little While: A Citizen's Guide to Hope in a Time of Fear* (New York: Basic Books, 2004), provided significant facts about Rosa Parks that aren't often included in the public portrayal of her. Douglas Brinkley's wonderful biography in the Penguin Lives series, *Rosa Parks* (New York: Viking, 2000), much of it based on interviews with Parks, gave us rich details of her life.

Anne's 1998 tour of Robben Island in Cape Town, South Africa, provided a background on Nelson Mandela's imprisonment and the communal effort to transform the prison experience into a forum for the creation of a new nation. Mandela's excellent and extensive autobiography, *Long Walk to Freedom* (New York: Back Bay Books, 1994), was the basis for his profile, along with the film produced by Jonathan Demme, *Mandela: Son of Africa, Father of a Nation* (New York: Palm Pictures, 1997).

Dr. Martin Luther King, Jr.'s "Letter from a Birmingham Jail" (reprinted in *The Impossible Will Take A Little*

While, above, as well as in many other sources) was our starting point for writing about the emergence of King's leadership. The first two volumes of Taylor Branch's trilogy on the civil rights movement, *Parting the Waters: America in the King Years 1954–63* (New York: Simon and Schuster, 1988), and *Pillar of Fire: America in the King Years 1963–65* (1998), gave a fascinating and intimate glimpse of the complex interplay of personalities and politics in the events in Montgomery and Birmingham. *Bearing the Cross: Martin Luther King, Jr., and the Southern Christian Leadership Conference,* by David J. Garrow (New York: Morrow, 1986) offered insights into Gandhi's influence on the development of Dr. Martin Luther King, Jr.'s nonviolent theories and strategies.

Charles Perkins's autobiography, *A Bastard Like Me* (Sydney: Ure Smith, 1975, o.p.), helped us understand Perkins's voice and experiences. *Charles Perkins: A Biography* by Peter Read (New York: Viking, 1990), filled in important biographical details.

Three key sources for information on César Chávez's life and work were *The Fight in the Fields: César Chávez and the Farmworkers Movement* by Susan Ferriss and Ricardo Sandoval (San Diego: Harcourt Brace & Company, 1997), a companion to the PBS documentary of the same name; *Chávez and the Farm Workers* (Boston: Beacon Press, 1975) by Ronald B. Taylor; and *César Chávez: Autobiography of La Causa* by Jacques E. Levy (New York: W.W. Norton & Company, Inc., 1975).

Muhammad Ali: His Life and Times by Thomas Hauser (New York: Simon and Schuster, 1991) provided a comprehensive introduction to the fighter. Written by Ali's doctor, Ferdie Pacheco, *Muhammad Ali: A View from the Corner* (New York: Carol Publishing, 1992) gave us an insider's perspective on Ali's rise to fame. *Redemption Song: Muhammad Ali and the Spirit of the Sixties* by Mike Marqusee (New York: Verso, 1999) related Ali to the political movements of the times.

Mairead Corrigan, Betty Williams by Richard Deutsch (Hauppauge, NY: Barron's, 1977) has a foreword by folk musician Joan Baez, an ally of Corrigan and Williams who performed at some of their protests. *Mairead Corrigan and Betty Williams: Making Peace in Northern Ireland* by Bettina Ling and Sarah Buscher (New York: Feminist Press, 1999) is part of the Women Changing the World series of children's books, which also includes a volume on Aung San Suu Kyi. We also drew extensively from contemporary newspaper reports from Ireland about the work of Corrigan and Williams.

Our key source for information on the Madres de la Plaza de Mayo was *Mothers of the Disappeared* (Boston: South End Press, 1989). Jo Fisher based the account on extensive interviews conducted in 1985 and 1987 with many of the surviving Mothers.

Aung San Suu Kyi's book, *Freedom from Fear and Other Writings* (New York: Penguin, 1991), includes forewords by Vaclav Havel and Desmond Tutu. We also consulted *The Lady: Aung San Suu Kyi, Nobel Laureate and Burma's Prisoner* by Barbara Victor (London: Faber and Faber, 1998).

Massacre in Beijing: China's Struggle for Democracy, edited by Donald Morrison (New York: Warner Books, 1989), gave an overview of the events of Tiananmen Square. *Voices from Tiananmen Square: Beijing Spring and the Democracy Movement* by Mok C. Yu (Montreal: Black Rose Books, 1990) provided first-hand testimonies from the people who were there. *Struggle for Tiananmen: Anatomy of the 1989 Mass Movement* by Nan Lin (Westport, CT: Praeger, 1990) added important political and cultural background information.

Two biographies of Archbishop Desmond Tutu were most helpful in assembling the facts of his life: *Tutu: Voice of the Voiceless* by Shirley DuBoulay (Grand Rapids: Eerdmans, 1998) and *Desmond Tutu: A Biography* by Stephen Gish (Westport, CT: Greenwood Press, 2004).

Three books were key in researching Václav Havel: *Václav Havel: The Authorized Biography* by Eda Kriseová (New York: St. Martin's Press, 1993); *A Velvet Revolution: Václav Havel and the Fall of Communism* by John Duberstein (Greensboro, NC: Morgan Reynolds, 2006); and *Václav Havel: A Political Tragedy in Six Acts* by John Keane (New York: Basic Books, 2000), which related Havel's political life to his love of theater.

We began researching Wangari Maathai online at the websites of the Nobel Peace Prize (www.nobelprize.org) and the Green Belt Movement (www.greenbeltmovement.org). On October 17, 2006, Anne and Perry attended an address given by Maathai at Syracuse University and had the opportunity to ask about the people and events that influenced her in developing a nonviolent approach. That speech and the fall 2006 release of her autobiography, *Unbowed* (New York: Alfred A. Knopf, 2006), gave details which added depth to the profile we had constructed.

Our information on global resistance to the invasion of Iraq came from a variety of online news sources and archives.

ACKNOWLEDGMENTS

This book wouldn't exist without the work of Margy Burns Knight and Mark Melnicove. The concept and proposal for what became *After Gandhi* was originally developed as a three-way collaboration with Anne. We acknowledge with gratitude the years of research and reflection which provided the foundation on which we built this book.

Editor Judy O'Malley fanned the spark that was the concept for the book until it ignited, and she tended the fire throughout its formation. Art Director Susan Sherman was an indispensible member of our team, contributing ideas that shaped the book's content as well as its design. The crew at Charlesbridge, especially Editorial Director Yolanda LeRoy, helped us tie up all the loose ends and bring the project to completion.

We thank our readers who provided invaluable insights and corrections: Chun Yu, author, who was a student at Beijing University involved in the Tiananmen Square Movement; and Nomakhosi Jenness, journalist, who escaped apartheid South Africa as a teenager and returned to work there post-apartheid.

This book grew with the help of our own group of future world-changers, the members of Gandhi Publishing: Dan Dorfman, Erika Joyce, Will Lenk, Caitlin Lowell, Devon Miller, Abdullahi Mohamed, Fazal Nabi, Danny Pang, Grania Power, Tess Tacka, Ellen Taffere, Gabe Terraccianao, Barbara VanDerburgh, and Lule Zequirian. These students from King Middle School in Portland, Maine, were our companions as we created this book. Self-selected in response to an invitation from school librarian Kelley McDaniel, they gathered for five sessions to listen to us present our ideas and process for the book at various stages of development and to respond with comments and questions. Over the year we worked on this book, they gave us inspiration, ideas, and much-needed guidance. We acknowledge with delight their contributions, as well as the pleasure we had working with them.

We thank staff member Cathy Flynn, other library staff and volunteers, the teachers who released the students for our meetings, and most of all Kelley McDaniel, who made Gandhi Publishing possible.

INDEX